Foundations of
LITERACY

Also available from Network Continuum

Foundations of Numeracy – Mercia Lee and Helen Yorke

Encouraging Reading – Susan Elkin

Flying Start with Literacy – Ros Bayley and Lyn Broadbent

Available from Continuum

Beginning Reading – Yola Center

100 Ideas for Teaching Communication, Language and Literacy – Susan Elkin

Foundations of
LITERACY

A balanced approach to language, listening
and literacy skills in the early years

Sue Palmer
and **Ros Bayley**

network
continuum

Continuum International Publishing Group
Network Continuum
The Tower Building   80 Maiden Lane, Suite 704
11 York Road   New York,
London   NY 10038
SE1 7NX

www.networkcontinuum.co.uk
www.continuumbooks.com

First published 2004
Revised 2005
Second edition 2007

© Sue Palmer and Ros Bayley 2008

British Library Cataloguing-in-Publication Data
A catalogue record for this book is available from the British Library.

ISBN: 9781847060891 (paperback)

Library of Congress Cataloging-in-Publication Data
A catalog record for this book is available from the Library of Congress.

Typeset by Fakenham Photosetting Limited, Fakenham, Norfolk
Printed and bound in Great Britain by Ashford Colour Press Ltd, Gosport, Hampshire

Contents

About the authors

Sue Palmer, a former primary headteacher, has written more than 200 books and educational television programmes on aspects of literacy. She writes regularly for the *Times Educational Supplement* and *Child Education*, provides in-service courses in schools, universities and LEAs throughout the UK and acts as a literacy consultant to the DfES, many educational publishers and the BBC. She has contributed to several National Literacy Strategy training packages and advised on the CBeebies *Razzledazzle* programmes and BBC Schools *Listen and Play* radio series. Her most recent books, *Toxic Childhood: how the modern world is damaging our children and what we can do about it* and *Detoxing Childhood* (both Orion Publishing) are aimed at parents as well as teachers (see also www.suepalmer.co.uk).

Following an extensive career as an early years teacher, **Ros Bayley** now works as an early years consultant, trainer and storyteller. Throughout her career she has devoted much time to developing children's creativity and imagination through story, puppetry, music, dance and dramatic play, and has shared her strategies with practitioners both in the UK and abroad. She also has a passionate interest in the development of literacy skills and has written a wide range of resources for foundation stage practitioners. She was a contributor to the DfES *Curriculum Guidance for the Foundation Stage*, and has recently completed *Flying Start with Literacy* (with Lynn Broadbent), a parents' guide to the *Foundations of Literacy* approach.

Authors' note

This is not an academic book, so we have not included academic references to the research which often underpins our thinking. However, anyone requiring a specific reference should write to Sue Palmer and Ros Bayley, c/o Network Continuum, The Tower Building, 11 York Road, London, SE1 7NX and we'll do our best to provide further information.

Acknowledgements

The authors would like to thank the many early years practitioners, primary teachers and other professionals who have helped in the compilation of this book, throughout the UK and Europe. Special thanks are due to Pie Corbett (literacy), Lynn Broadbent (early years), Linda Caroe (music), Clare Mills and Philippa Crooks (speech and language) and the late David Weikart of High Scope, who have contributed so much to our understanding and given us many new ideas. We are also particularly grateful to the following people for advice and/or support: Margaret Donaldson and Jessie Reid; Roger Beard; Greg Brooks; Anne Locke; Diane Hofkins; Marion Nash; Julia Bond; Carole Kimberley; David Mills; Sue Moncur and Janet King; Jane Oates of the Royal College of Speech and Language Therapists; Peter Brinton, Mandy Lawrence, Catherine Williams, Clare Taylor, Jo Small and Pat Hart of Roskear Primary School, Cornwall; Hazel Mills and the children and staff of Arkwright Nursery and Lady Bay School in Nottingham; Mayer-Johnson for the use of the PCS symbol card on page 18 and TTS Group who loaned resources for photographs and trialling. And many thanks to those people in High Places who must remain anonymous but whose advice was enormously helpful.

We should also like to thank the National Literacy Trust for bringing us together and *Child Education* magazine for commissioning the series of articles that inspired the book. Finally, many thanks to Lynda Lawrence for the use of her email; Michaela Morgan for permission to use action rhymes co-written with Sue Palmer; John Redman for photography; Bridget Gibbs, Sarah Nunn and Neil Hawkins, and Ulrike Vaughan for, day by day, holding the project together.

Introduction

The importance of language in education cannot be exaggerated. It is the bedrock on which all formal learning is based, not least the learning of literacy skills. *Foundations of Literacy* is an ongoing project aimed at providing the best possible basis for young children's language and literacy learning. It has been developed in response to concern among early years practitioners that, in a multimedia world, children's language and listening skills are less well-honed than in the past. At the same time, the 'academic' demands of early education have increased – so, as oral language development has become ever more important, less and less time has been available for it.

This book is offered as a starting point for practitioners who are anxious to redress this balance. In consultation with a wide range of experts in early years, music, literacy and language development, we have devised a seven-stranded approach, based on successful UK and European practice. For each strand we have defined:

- key skills, concepts and knowledge that can be used in the pre-school education of 3 to 6 year olds (these are described on the left-hand page of each spread)

- examples of the types of activity that should develop these skills, concepts and knowledge (these are given on the right-hand pages of each spread).

These activities are designed to be attractive to young children, but by their nature are generally adult-initiated. However, as the Effective Provision of Pre-School Education (EPPE) project has found (see Further reading), the most effective learning occurs when there is a balance of adult-directed and child-initiated activities. We have therefore also tried to illustrate throughout the book how learning from group activities can be extended into child-initiated play.

As illustrated on pages 120–30, very many of the developmental milestones and early learning goals in the *Practice Guidance for the Early Years Foundation Stage* in England are covered by the activities recommended in *Foundations of Literacy*, particularly those in:

- **personal, social and emotional** development (especially Chapters 1 and 2)

- **creative** development (especially Chapters 3, 4 and 5)

- **physical** development (especially Chapters 3 and 7).

And, of course, this book as a whole covers – often in greater detail and with many practical suggestions – the goals in the **communication, language and literacy** section. There is, however, a slight change of emphasis.

We believe that over-emphasis on the following goals has been instrumental in increasing the formalization of early years, and generating inappropriate practice:

- hear and say sounds in words in the order in which they occur

- use phonic knowledge to write simple regular words and make phonetically plausible attempts at more complex words

- read a range of familiar and common words and simple sentences independently

- ... begin to form simple sentences, sometimes using punctuation

- ... form recognizable letters, most of which are correctly formed.

In a well-organized and resourced foundation setting, many children will achieve these four goals 'naturally' by the age of 6 through their own emergent reading and writing activities. However, children who do not achieve them naturally are unlikely to benefit from an early emphasis on formal learning. They are the very children who, in the pre-school years, need a greater emphasis on language and listening skills and the physical skills required for handwriting. The *Foundations of Literacy* curriculum provides such an emphasis, as well as activities to develop literacy skills and understanding, which should allow most children to achieve the goals easily by the age of 6 or 7 years old.

To change the emphasis in this way is not by any means to recommend a 'dumbing down' of early years practice. Indeed, the practitioners who have been trialling these ideas say they have never worked harder! The *Foundations of Literacy* approach is very rigorous and structured, with a strong theoretical basis – it simply recognizes that there are many other skills to be developed in the early years if formal teaching is eventually to succeed. These factors have long been recognized in successful European countries such as Sweden, Finland and Switzerland, where children do not start school until they are 7 years old, after three years in pre-school following a highly structured, orally based curriculum.

This begs the question of whether we in the UK should delay the onset of 'formal' literacy teaching. Clearly, different children in different schools will acquire the skills, concepts and knowledge of *Foundations of Literacy* at different rates. For instance, children from language-rich backgrounds, where many *FoL* activities are familiar before they even arrive in a pre-school, may well be quite secure in all seven strands by the end of the Reception year. For others, it may be that another full year is needed to cover the *FoL* curriculum, and formal literacy should not begin until Year 2. Our feeling is that *most* children would benefit from following the curriculum we describe until they are at least 6 years old. In England, that would probably be the beginning of Year 1, term 2.

Some children in any group will, as we have already mentioned, start reading and writing before their peers under their own steam. They should, of course, on no account be held back – practitioners should encourage and celebrate their achievements and give help and support where appropriate. These children will then form a 'top group' once formal learning starts. But we're sure that they too would benefit from increased attention to speaking, listening, music and social development, and a more informal approach to their interest in reading and writing, until they are at least 6 years old.

The *Foundations of Literacy* curriculum is in this way consistent with the goals of the Early Years Foundation Stage and can therefore be adopted in nurseries, Reception and Year 1 classes in English primary schools. It is also consistent with early years policy and practice in Scotland and Northern Ireland. In Wales, the new *Foundation Phase* for 3 to 7 year olds is utterly in keeping with the *Foundations of Literacy* philosophy. We firmly believe that such an approach will, in the long run, lead to an improvement in standards of reading and writing because fewer children will encounter early failure, spending the rest of their school careers following 'catch-up' programmes which, sadly, do not seem to work.

As we said at the beginning, *Foundations of Literacy* is an ongoing project and this book is merely a starting point. We hope practitioners will use it to develop practice in strengthening the linguistic, cognitive, physical and emotional foundations for literacy learning in the children in their care.

Sue Palmer and Ros Bayley

Chapter One

Learning to **listen**

Learning to listen

There can be little doubt that, in terms of literacy, and perhaps all school-based education, the most fundamental skill of all is *listening*. Unless children can listen, discriminatively and with growing attention, they will be slow to understand and slow to talk. As they grow older, they'll have difficulty relating and attending to their teachers, which easily leads to behavioural problems and disaffection, blighting the ability to learn throughout their school career.

For many years, it's been clear to early years practitioners that, in an increasingly noise-filled world, children's listening skills are being steadily eroded. Television, video and computer games now fill homes with daylong noise. Shared family mealtimes, once a daily opportunity for conversational speaking and listening, have given way to television-dominated grazing. Nowadays, even the pushchairs face outwards, so parents don't even chat to their children as they wheel them down the road; but with the level of traffic noise these days, would the children hear anyway? Gradually, and scarcely without noticing it has happened, our society has stopped teaching its children how to listen.

It is, therefore, extremely important that, as soon as possible, we make learning to listen (and its counterpart, learning to speak – see Chapter 2) a major focus of attention. For children from 'language-poor' backgrounds, with little experience of listening and being listened to, this may not be easy. It requires informed, structured attention over an extended period. We therefore need to take our lead from colleagues in Europe, who provide structured listening skills programmes, starting when children are 3 and continuing until they are 6 or 7.

Discrimination of sounds

Many children need help in the most basic listening skill of all – discriminating a foreground sound against background noise. It's what children must learn to do in their first year of life, in order to learn language: single out their mother's voice from the irrelevant noise of their surroundings. In the past, this went without saying, but in an increasingly noisy world we can't assume it will happen naturally.

Indeed, speech and language therapist Sally Ward, who conducted a long-term study at the end of the last century, found a disturbing deterioration in babies' ability to discriminate significant sounds. In 1984, 20 per cent of the 9-month-old infants she tested were unable to listen selectively; by 1999, the proportion had risen to 40 per cent. It's hugely important, therefore, that as soon as children arrive in a pre-school setting, we provide activities to help them develop this essential skill.

Once able to single out significant sound, children must learn to discriminate and attend to a widening range of auditory information, through plenty of musical activities, 'listening walks' and games. The ability to listen discriminately is vital if children are to achieve the fine discrimination between speech sounds needed for clear articulation and phonological awareness (see Chapter 6).

A crucial aspect of playing listening games, such as those suggested opposite, is to increase the confidence and skills of those children who find listening particularly difficult. Children who seem unable to listen discriminately in active games need opportunities to play the game again in a smaller group. In 'circle games' they should sit close to an adult who can give them additional help. Less skilled listeners also need plenty of opportunities for one-to-one interaction with an adult in a quiet environment (see page 26).

Dodgems develops children's ability to single out a foreground sound against background noise.

> **A child who is consistently baffled by the sort of activities suggested opposite may have a problem with hearing. If you are concerned, seek specialist help immediately.**

Foreground sound against background noise

Dodgems
Familiarize children with a particular sound (e.g. clapping, tambourine, bell), which is the signal both to 'start' and 'stop'. On hearing the 'start' signal, children pretend to be cars, speeding around (avoiding each other!) and making an appropriate noise. Make the sound again to signal 'stop', and wait a few moments for all the children to respond. Give praise for recognizing the signal, and continue the game.

Traffic lights
Explain to the children that they are going to be vehicles driving along the road and that they are to respond to the traffic lights as quickly as possible! Further explain that you will shout out a colour, and that when you do, they must respond with the appropriate action. For example, when you shout 'amber' they are to bend down and touch the floor, when you shout 'red' they must stop and stay completely still, and when you shout 'green' they can begin to move again. They particularly enjoy this game if you give out paper plates for them to use as steering wheels!

Statues
Play some lively music with a strong beat and explain to the children that they can dance to the music, but that when you shout 'stop' over the top of the music, they must freeze like statues. Go on to explain that when you shout 'go', they can begin to dance again. If you prefer, you can use musical instruments for the 'stop' and 'go' signals!

Widening the range of aural discrimination

Listening walks
Take children on a walk around the school building or grounds, or out in the local area. Explain that you are going to listen for any sounds, such as cars, birds, people talking, and so on. Tell the children they have to walk very quietly and if they hear a sound, put up their hand, whereupon everyone must stop. Invite the child to say what sound they heard. Once they get good at this, your walk will be frequently interrupted, so get them to stop every so often instead and 'collect' as many sounds as they can hear. You can integrate a 'listening section' into any outing.

Spot the sound
Choose a number of items with recognizable sounds, for example: a music box, a ticking clock, an automatic timer, or sounds recorded on tape. Gather the children together and explain that, while they close their eyes, you are going to hide a 'sound' somewhere in the classroom. On your signal, they have to listen hard and guess (a) what it is and (b) where it's hidden.

Who is it?
Sit one child on a chair with their back to the rest of the children. Explain to the children that if you tap them on the head they are to say, '*Who is it?*' The child on the chair attempts to identify the voices of the children as they ask the question. Whenever they play the game, they can try to break their own record.

Games on tape
There are many commercially available games using taped sounds for use during child-initiated learning, for example, 'Sound Lotto' activities (see Recommended resources). It's also fun to make your own, using sounds familiar to the children, especially snippets of their own voices for them to guess who's who.

Social listening

Listening in one-to-one conversation involves making frequent eye contact with the speaker. In a group situation, such as when a practitioner is talking to a number of children, eye contact is even more important, as it signals to the speaker that the listeners are attending to his/her words. Young children with poor language skills particularly need to attend to the speaker's face, as facial expression provides support for the spoken words.

However, many children these days find it difficult to make eye contact, perhaps because in homes where television is constantly switched on, people look at the screen rather than each other. The ability to look someone in the eye must therefore be developed as early as possible.

Other specific social skills include:

- **attending to the speaker** (e.g. focusing, not fidgeting, ignoring distractions – gradually building up attention span)
- **remembering and responding** to what is said
- **turn-taking**.

While it's easy and natural for children to focus attention when they are emotionally engaged, they must also learn to follow social conventions in less interesting contexts. This involves awareness of what is required and opportunities to practise behaviour in non-threatening, pleasurable circumstances.

It also involves seeing plenty of models of acceptable behaviour – and that means you! In class and group discussion, and when talking with children individually, it's important to demonstrate how a good listener behaves. In a busy classroom this isn't always easy, so efficient organizational and management techniques are extremely important (see page 18).

Circle time is an opportunity to model attentive listening. In the early stages keep circles small (6-8 children). As they build up the capacity to attend, gradually build up the size of the circle.

Eye contact

Here's looking at you, kid

Teach children how to make eye contact by using it as a selection device. For instance, when it's time to go and get their coats to go home, tell the children '*I'm not going to say your name when it's time to get your coat today, I'm going to **look** at you*'. This is usually guaranteed to ensure all eyes are fixed on yours, dying to make contact! Once they're familiar with this technique, choose an individual child to be the one who makes eye contact ('*Sophie's going to be the "looker" today*').

Welcome!

Make children want to look and listen to you with daily compliments! As they arrive in school, have an adult 'greeter', whose job is to look each new arrival in the eye and say something nice, for example:

> *I love your hair-band today!*
> *What a happy smiling face – you brighten my day!*
> *That's a gorgeous red jumper. Is it new?*

Encourage children to respond if they wish.

Circle time

Many circle time activities encourage eye contact and turn-taking, from 'passing a look (or a wink) around the circle' to games like those below. For details of many 'circle time' resources for early years see Recommended resources.

Social attention

Signal!

You will need: a favourite soft toy and a bell, whistle or musical instrument.
Sit the children in a circle and explain that the toy is going to be taken for a ride around the circle. When the bell rings, whoever's holding the toy must stop as quickly as possible and hold it perfectly still. As the toy is passed around the circle, the children should follow it with their eyes. As they get better at responding to the signal, increase the challenge by having them pass the toy in the opposite direction when the bell rings.

Mystery object

You will need: a mystery object; for example, a toy car or a piece of Lego.
Put the mystery object into an envelope. Explain you will whisper in the ear of the child next to you, telling what's in the envelope. They then whisper to the next child, and so on around the circle. When everyone's had a turn, open the envelope – have they named the object correctly?

Toys go for a spin

You will need: soft toys and musical instruments.
Explain that the children, in a circle, are going to pass one of the toys around until there is a signal. Agree with the children what the signals will mean, for example, the whistle means they must carry the toy to the person directly opposite them; the tambourine means give the toy to a boy; the shaker – give it to a girl. Let them suggest what should happen on the signals. As they become more skilled, try having more than one toy moving around at once.

Developing aural attention span

Listening games and activities should aim at the gradual and incremental development of children's aural attention span. For children whose early life has been filled with *visual* stimuli on screens and who are also used to being able to 'rewind' at will if they don't catch something first time, this is not always easily achieved. However, it's well worth the effort. A recent Ofsted report (see Further reading) on the education of 6 year olds in Finland, Denmark and England, noted that children in the Scandinavian countries – where listening is targeted in this way from the age of 3 – were more attentive, concentrated for longer, and had a higher boredom threshold than English children. They were also considerably better behaved.

One important element in encouraging children to listen is to ensure that what you have to say is worth listening to! Over-exposure of your voice for behaviour management or organisation can lead some children to switch off. Look for ways of substituting other modes of communication wherever possible, for instance:

- instead of using your voice to attract children's attention, devise a physical signal such as holding one arm in the air, and ask children to respond by quietly signalling back.

- if there are routines or rules you frequently need to repeat, make a picture poster of them that you can just point to. Symbols such as PCS (*Picture Communication System*) are available commercially – see Recommended resources.

- for children who constantly need reminding how to behave in a group situation, make visual cue cards that you or another adult can hold up. Or use physical signs, such as Makaton – see Recommended resources.

- provide a daily timetable with visual cues for each element of each particular session, so children can refer to it when they come in, and throughout the day – then they always know what to expect.

Once children have developed a reasonable level of attention, it also helps to use audio resources – poems, songs and short stories on tape or CD (the latter is preferable, because tracks are so much easier to access, especially if you have a remote control). There are also BBC school radio programmes, such as *Listen and Play*, appropriate for 3–6-year-old children (see Recommended Resources). These resources bring other voices into the classroom and provide a powerful motivation for children to listen carefully first time around, especially if you provide a focus by suggesting they are to listen for some specific sound or words.

Visual cue cards can be useful for behaviour management.

Children who, despite a carefully planned course of listening activities, are still unable to concentrate may have Attention Deficit Disorder, and should be referred to an educational psychologist for assessment. However, while there is no doubt that this condition exists, we believe many children may be falsely diagnosed simply because of poorly developed listening skills and/or too few opportunities for active outdoor play.

Spinning bottle

You will need: a plastic bottle.
Sit a small group of children in a circle and explain that you are going to spin the bottle and then shout out someone's name. Go on to explain that the person whose name is called has got to try and pick up the bottle before it stops spinning. Call the children's names at random until everyone has had a go.

Sausages

Choose one of the children's favourite story books and select a word that appears with reasonable frequency, for example, the name of the main character. Explain to the children that you're going to read the story and that they must listen very carefully for your chosen word. Further explain that each time they hear it, they are to shout 'sausages!' Once they've got the hang of it, select another word and encourage the children to generate ideas for what they will shout when they hear it.

Toss the beanbag

You will need: a beanbag for each child and a bowl, bucket or hoop.
Sit the children in a circle with the bowl, bucket or hoop in the middle. Give out the beanbags and explain that on a given signal, they are to toss their beanbag into the receptacle in the middle of the circle. Explain that they will need to listen really carefully for 'their' signal – this could be their name or a number you have given them. Call out the names or numbers at random until all the beanbags have been thrown into the receptacle. Talk through the skills and behaviours that are needed in order for the group to accomplish the task.

Quick responses

You will need: three different musical instruments.
The object of this game is for the children to execute a different movement to the sound of each of the musical instruments. Negotiate how they will move to each signal, for example, *'Jump up and down when you hear the tambourine, stamp your feet when you hear the drum and clap your hands when you hear the whistle.'*

Jack in a box

Ask the children if they know what a 'Jack in a box' is, and talk about why it is called that. Explain that you are going to play a game where everyone is a Jack in a box. Ask the children to curl up as small as they can and tell them that they cannot explode out of the 'box' until you lift the lid – you can do this by calling the children's names at random. Further explain that once they have exploded, they must try to remain completely still and quiet until all the other children have 'come out of their boxes'. If anyone is finding the task really difficult, get the children to generate ideas for how they could help this person to remain still!

Shooting stars

You will need: a cut-out cardboard star for each child with either a number or picture in the middle.
Sit the children on chairs in a circle and make sure that there is one spare chair. Give out the stars and explain to the children that they have to listen very carefully for their number or picture to be called. Tell them that as soon as they hear their number or picture called out, they are to move to the spare chair as quickly as possible. The next person to be called moves to the chair that they have vacated. Carry on until everyone has changed seats. Talk with the children about the behaviour and skills that are involved in carrying out this game quickly and effectively.

Music and stories

The suggestions in Chapter 3 (Music, movement and memory) and Chapter 4 (Storytime!) provide many more opportunities for developing attention span.

Worth a thought

Do we sometimes inadvertently contribute to poor attention? A teaching assistant recently reported this conversation with a child with 'attention deficit' for whom she had responsibility:

TA: *Why do you never listen to what Mrs Williams [the teacher] says?*
Child: *There's no point. You'll tell me later anyway.*

Developing auditory memory

While developing aural attention span helps children to attend and concentrate, developing auditory memory helps them to learn. At all stages, but particularly in the early years, auditory memory seems to be bound up with kinesthetic learning, and among the first sequences of sound children learn are rhythmic chants. We have therefore devoted an entire chapter to Music, movement and memory, and the suggestions here should be read alongside Chapter 3.

From as early as possible, attention should be paid to helping children keep a **steady beat**, and every opportunity should be taken to use **action rhymes and songs** as a medium for learning.

Auditory memory may be employed on a short- or long-term basis. For instance, on a day-to-day basis we need short-term auditory memory to hold a phone number in mind long enough to dial it; we need long-term auditory memory for immediate recall of our own phone number, address, date of birth and so on. The games and activities provided opposite are mostly about developing the short-term memory skills underpinning verbal comprehension, phonetic analysis of words and other elementary aspects of literacy.

However, children also need opportunities to develop long-term auditory memory skills. **Learning songs and rhymes by heart** is therefore an important part of early childhood education, and once children have reached a level of language development appropriate for a 3 year old (see Appendix 1), we should be aiming to help them learn at least one new rhyme a week. In addition, Chapter 4 suggests ways of helping children internalize written language patterns through learning by heart during frequent and regular *Storytime!* activities.

The **Sound in Sequence** activity can be adapted as appropriate for the development level of the group.

> Watch out for children whose general listening skills (i.e. those covered on previous pages) seem to develop satisfactorily, but who have trouble with short-term auditory memory activities. This may be an indicator of specific learning difficulties. Children should be referred to the special needs co-ordinator for screening for dyslexia.

Auditory memory

Holiday!

You will need: some pictures of different modes of transport.

Sit the children in a circle with the picture cards face down in the middle of the circle. Explain to the children that you are going to pass an object around the circle and that when you shout 'Stop', or blow the whistle, the person holding the object is to choose a picture card and say, 'When I went on holiday I went by... (names vehicle on card)'. The child hands the picture card to you. They then carry on passing the object around, until you shout 'Stop' again and a second card is selected. The child repeats, 'When I went on holiday I went by... (names first vehicle), and.... (names vehicle selected)'. Continue, with each child attempting to recall the full string of forms of transport.

Mystery bag

You will need: a feely bag and an interesting object to place inside it.

Tell the children that they are to guess what is inside the feely bag and give them several alternatives. Pass the bag around the circle so that each child can make a guess from the alternatives given. When everyone has had their turn, ask the children to recall who guessed what and who guessed the same as them. The mystery object can then be identified!

Ted's walk

Make up a short story about Ted (or other favourite soft toy) going for a walk. Start off by setting the scene, for example, 'One bright sunny day, Ted decided to go for a walk. He walked down the road towards the shops and the first thing he saw was....'. Each child chooses one thing that Ted saw. When everyone has had a turn, see how many things the children can recall.

Long, tall Sally

Say the following rap, and each time you say it add one more thing until the children cannot remember any more:

> When long, tall Sally was walking down the alley well who do you think she saw?
> When long, tall Sally was walking down the alley well this is who she saw....

The children generate ideas for who Sally saw, and then repeat the rhyme, adding one more thing each time.

Shopping bag

You will need: a shopping bag and a variety of objects.

Sit the children in a circle and place the objects in the middle. The children take it in turns to select an item of shopping to put into the bag. As each object is placed in the bag, recite together, 'We went shopping and we bought....'. Continue until the children cannot remember any more. Play this game at regular intervals and encourage them to work together to beat their own record.

Movement directions

The children suggest different ways in which they could move and then you choose some of their ideas and give movement directions, firstly one at a time, then two at a time and then three at a time and so on. For example, 'Jump, touch the floor and then sit down'. The children experiment to see how many instructions they can remember

Sounds in sequence

You will need: two sets of small instruments (e.g. drum, rattle, triangle, shaker, chime bar) and a screen, or, ideally, a puppet theatre with curtains.

Keep one set of instruments behind the screen and play two of them or, as the children become more accomplished, three, four or five in sequence. Place the instruments down in sequence, and remove any unused instruments. Place a full set of instruments in front of the screen and ask children to identify the instruments played and place them in sequence. Then remove the screen. When the screen is removed, the children will have immediate feedback about the accuracy of their choice. Talk about any wrong choices and why they might have happened. Gradually establish a culture of confidence in responding and lack of fear or shame about being perceived as 'wrong'.

Supporting children's listening

The activities suggested on the previous pages are merely a beginning. If children are really to become active listeners, we must help them use these listening skills in their own child-initiated activities. We have to set up a 'listening culture' within which children can grow and develop as effective listeners.

- **Be a good listener**. Young children learn by listening, watching and copying, so we must be good role models. Listening is an active process requiring our full participation, and when children experience the power of being listened to, they learn by example. What we do is much more important than what we say, and as we interact with children throughout the daily routine, we must take advantage of the many opportunities that arise to demonstrate the behaviours of a good listener.

- **Be aware of what good listening involves**. Many practitioners are very supportive of children's listening, but because they do it intuitively, are not really aware of what works best and why. If we take time to reflect on what seems to work and what doesn't, we can use this awareness to inform our listening in the future.

- **Be a genuine listener**. When children are playing, we need to involve ourselves sensitively in their play and listen really carefully to the things they have to say. It is not enough simply to look interested, we need to be interested in the things that are important to them, engaging them in conversations about their projects, their interests, their families and their communities. We need to consult about what's important to them and take their opinions into serious consideration. By doing this, we show them how a genuine listener behaves.

- **Demonstrate the value of listening**. As adults, we can help children see that good listeners achieve in ways that aren't available to people who don't know how to listen. When children are involved in conflicts over space, friends or resources, we can help them listen to each other and resolve their difficulties, thus developing essential skills for life and learning.

- **Help children make links**. During periods of child-initiated learning, we can sensitively remind children of the skills they have been developing at group times and to help them to use these skills as and when appropriate. Where possible, the resources that have been used for the games and activities should be available during periods of child-initiated learning, so that children can consolidate their skills and practise and build on what they have already learned.

- **Provide a suitable environment**. Are there quiet places where children can go to listen to each other, listen to stories and play musical instruments? If we provide enough open-ended materials (e.g. wooden frames and plenty of drapes) the children can create dens and little secret areas where attentive listening can take place. If at all possible we should also provide a performance area where children can perform for each other and learn how to be a respectful member of an audience. If it is not possible to do so inside, space for such a purpose can usually be found outside!

Good listening does not happen by accident. It is a learnable skill, and with a consistent approach we can help all children become better listeners.

Further suggestions for activities and more detailed background on the skills and concepts involved in effective listening can now be found in Sue's book *You Can Teach Your Class to Listen: Ages 4–7* (Scholastic, 2007).

Chapter Two

Time to **talk**

Time to talk

Talk matters. We need it to communicate and co-exist with others, to explore and express our experiences, to proclaim our needs, hopes, fears and passions. We need it to think and learn – not least to learn the skills of literacy. '*Reading and writing*,' said educationist James Britton, '*float on a sea of talk.*'

How worrying then, that over the past quarter century many children's facility with spoken language seems to have steadily declined. The social and environmental factors mentioned in the last chapter (television, computers, the decline of family mealtimes) have all played a part, but there are many other contributory factors. Fewer extended families, changes in working patterns, even the advent of central heating (meaning families no longer need to huddle in the same room for warmth!) have resulted in adults spending less time than ever before with their children. And this means less of the interactive language that children need to develop speech. Both the Chief Inspector of Schools and the Director of the Basic Skills Agency have expressed concern about the level of young children's language on entry to school.

It's even more worrying that, while children's speaking and listening skills waned, attention to these skills in early years settings was also eroded. In England, many practitioners found the emphasis on tests, targets, and pencil-and-paper work in Key Stage 1 had a knock-on effect into Reception and pre-school provision (and, despite apparently less formal regimes, this has often also been the case in Scotland, Wales and Northern Ireland). In the early years of the twenty-first century, children have been expected to knuckle down to formal work earlier and earlier, and the time for developing oral language, like the time for play, has grown ever smaller.

It's up to practitioners to make the development of spoken language one of the highest priorities of pre-school education. As well as resisting pressure to introduce pencil-and-paper work, this means finding ways to support the development of oral language skills. This chapter offers some starting points.

Compensating for language delay

There is a well-established developmental model for language acquisition: **listen**, **imitate**, **innovate**, **invent**. Children are 'programmed' to learn naturally – given enough examples of interactive language on which to base their learning. Sadly, for many children this is not always the case at home.

Another worrying factor is the research finding that, as children's language skills have deteriorated, practitioners' expectations have also decreased. 'Normal' language development is outlined in Appendix 1. We should start with the expectation that all children can achieve these levels of speech, and give concerted help to those who start from a lower baseline.

Children with language delay need as much one-to-one talk as possible, preferably a daily 'focused talk' session with an adult. One way to tackle this is to give each adult a list of up to six of the most needy children, with each of whom they must spend five to ten minutes each day targeting language development. Adults can then just pick up on what's happening naturally in the setting, addressing children's language in context and at the appropriate level.

Talk during child-initiated activities is often particularly productive, as the more contextualized language is, the easier it is to learn. When cooking, playing, making something or engaged in role play, children can use all their senses to support new vocabulary or language structures. However, you have to be very careful and sensitive when intervening in this way (see Talk during child-initiated activities, page 28).

In addition, of course, we need to ensure that all opportunities for talk with all children are exploited as productively as possible and to include regular group 'talk time' sessions throughout the day.

All children respond to puppets and soft toys.

Given focused attention within an overall structured language curriculum, many children with language delay make rapid progress. Those who don't should be referred to a speech and language therapist for assessment. They may well benefit from small-group work using a programme such as *Spirals* (see Recommended resources).

Expand sentences

This mirrors the way parents initially introduce language to their children – by picking up on what the child says, and expanding on it, for example:

Child: *Daddy gone.*
Adult: *Yes. Daddy's gone home.*

When expanding a sentence, take care not to expand it too much – just enough to give the child an achievable model.

Provide alternatives

If you're not sure what the child means, try to provide simple alternatives, for example:

Child: *Doggy naughty goed out.*
Adult: *Oh, the doggy was naughty, was he? Did he run away? Or did mummy send him out?*

Again, try to keep the language you use simple enough for the child to pick up in a reply. And avoid offering 'yes/no' or single word replies. Ideally, you want the child to have to answer in longer sentences, picking up on the language you have provided.

Model pole-bridging talk

'Pole-bridging talk' is the sort of running commentary young children often use to accompany their actions (see also page 28). Rather than asking the child, *'What are you doing?'* sit alongside and comment, *'I see you're playing in the sand. I think I'll play too – I'm making a castle. I have to heap up the sand like this....'* providing plenty of silences for the child to respond or join in, if they want to. Pitch your talk at an appropriate level for the child – short clear sentences and plenty of simple nouns and verbs. As well as providing clear language models, this approach has the advantage that it often encourages children to start speaking themselves, often picking up on the structures and vocabulary you have provided.

Give plenty of time

Ask questions sparingly (see page 29) but when you do, or when you ask oblique questions (e.g. *'I wonder what that's called?'*) give plenty of time for the child to answer. Count up to 15 in your head, and then, if appropriate, offer to say it again. Waiting for a response can feel strange, and adults often feel embarrassed for the child, but many children do need plenty of processing time. You may have to tackle this issue with the other children too. For instance, if a child with language delay is taking a long time to respond during circle time, and the others are beginning to get restive, explain that *'Sometimes we all need some extra thinking time. In our circle, we wait politely for people to think what they want to say. And it helps if we stay quiet, too.'*

Offer visual support

Children with language delay often find visual support particularly helpful – so whenever possible support what you're saying with pictures, photographs and actual artefacts that they can hold. In fact, this technique helps all children, including those speaking English as an additional language. Some children also find symbols helpful, especially for more abstract words. These can be either pictorial symbols, such as PCS (see Recommended resources), or physical signs, such as Makaton signs.

Use puppets and soft toys

Puppets and soft toys add excitement and engagement to learning activities for all children, but can be especially useful with shy children and those with language delay. A child who finds talking to adults difficult will often 'open up' to a puppet or soft toy.

Talk during child-initiated activities

Talk during child-initiated activities helps children absorb new vocabulary and language structures easily, as there is a direct, concrete link between what they are doing and what you are saying. A self-chosen activity is also likely to be a motivating one for the child, which again makes learning more productive. Practitioners should therefore take every opportunity to engage all children in talk during periods of child-initiated learning.

However, while sensitive interaction with children at play is one of the most important skills of the early years practitioner, it is also one of the most subtle. Most of us, anxious to extend children's learning, have gone rushing into a play situation, only to find that the children have all got up and walked away! When approaching a child or children with a view to talk:

● stand back and look carefully at what is going on

● tune into what they are saying and/or doing, then quietly sit down and begin to play with some of the materials and equipment they are using

● once they're comfortable with your presence, engage in some 'self-talk' (see Pole-bridging talk below) describing what you are doing – talking to yourself rather than directly addressing the child

● usually, within a short space of time children will begin to respond to your self-talk, and once this has happened you can begin to extend both their play and their language.

Pole-bridging talk

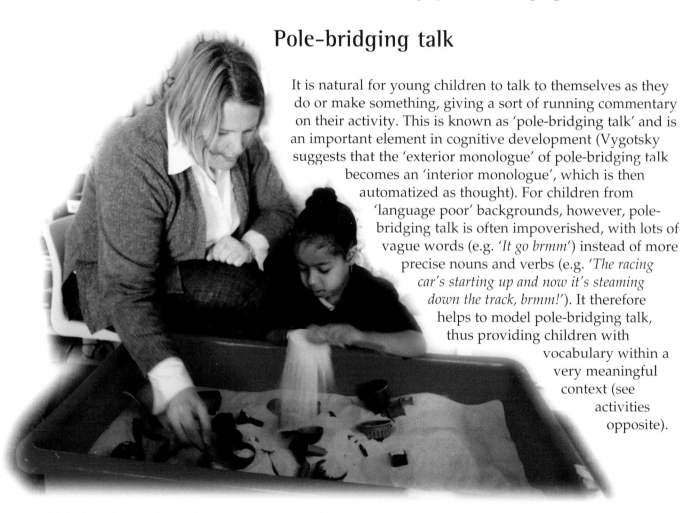

It is natural for young children to talk to themselves as they do or make something, giving a sort of running commentary on their activity. This is known as 'pole-bridging talk' and is an important element in cognitive development (Vygotsky suggests that the 'exterior monologue' of pole-bridging talk becomes an 'interior monologue', which is then automatized as thought). For children from 'language poor' backgrounds, however, pole-bridging talk is often impoverished, with lots of vague words (e.g. *'It go brmm'*) instead of more precise nouns and verbs (e.g. *'The racing car's starting up and now it's steaming down the track, brmm!'*). It therefore helps to model pole-bridging talk, thus providing children with vocabulary within a very meaningful context (see activities opposite).

Pole-bridging talk can provide models of language within a motivating and meaningful context.

> **For ideas and support in developing child-initiated learning see the book *First Hand Experience: what matters to children – an alphabet of learning from the real world* (see Recommended resources).**

Follow the children's lead

Follow children's leads and take turns with them. When deeply engaged in activities, children usually have a clear sense of purpose and a well-defined pattern of thinking. It is when adults tap into this that the most productive talk takes place. Any attempt to introduce another agenda can only result in frustration and lost opportunities.

Be conversational

Use their comments as conversational openers. Listen carefully to children and **repeat** back what they say. This gives value to what they have said and encourages them to keep talking, for example:

Child: *This car go fast...fast...very fast.*
Adult: *This car goes very, very fast.*
Child: *That 'cause it racing car.*
Adult: *That's because it's a racing car. Would you like to drive a racing car?*

Avoid the 'Spanish Inquisition'

Ask questions sparingly. Questions can put children on the spot. If they don't know the answer, or if they don't have the vocabulary or facility with language to answer, they often just freeze up. Tentative language can often be more effective: for example, *'I wonder why the sand did that…'*.

Seek enlightenment

One type of questioning that is often successful, however, is a display of genuine curiosity. Rather than asking questions like a teacher, ask them like an equal, for instance, asking children how they did something or asking for their help. This less direct, social questioning shows that you are interested in and respect their ideas, and can also develop their ideas.

Expand and extend

Expand and extend on what the children are doing. This can be thought of as a natural conversation technique where the adult introduces new ideas into the discussion in order to develop new ideas and vocabulary, for example:

Child: *When I went to the fair I went on the waltzers and it was great.*
Adult: *I went on the waltzers once, but I didn't like it.*
Child: *Why not? Why didn't you like it?*
Adult: *It made me dizzy.*
Child: *Why did it do that?* (You now have an opening to introduce new ideas and vocabulary.)

Model pole-bridging talk

This is one of the most valuable things we can do to develop both language and cognitive development, and it's very easy once you've practised a few times. There are many occasions when it is appropriate:

- during any play (indoor and out) or role play
- when you or a child are making something or engaged in any creative activity.

And there are two ways you can use the technique:

- Pole-bridge on behalf of the child or children you are sitting with. Describe their actions, thus providing them with the relevant vocabulary: for example, *'You are putting all of the dinosaurs in the bucket!'*
- Pole-bridge on behalf of yourself. Describe your own actions as you do something sitting alongside a child: for example, *'I think I'll make a necklace. I'm going to thread this piece of macaroni on to the string. I'll have to push it through the hole there. Now I'm pulling it along....'.*

But remember to leave plenty of long gaps between sections of your commentary, so that the child can join in or take over. And if the child is clearly irritated by your presence, stop!

Vocabulary development

Selected words and phrases related to topic work, storytime or other activities should be actively targeted each week, from Nursery through to Year 1. Each week, these should include words that:

- name, e.g. *postman, elephant*
- denote actions, e.g. *bring, carry*
- describe, e.g. *friendly, huge, gently*
- categorize, e.g. *jobs, animals* (and words that fall in the categories)
- denote position, e.g. *in, under, behind, between*
- denote sequence, e.g. *when, after*
- are used for reasoning, e.g. *if, but, because, so.*

It helps to make a poster of current target words, so that all adults in the setting are constantly reminded of them and make an effort to bring them into general conversation.

It can take many exposures to a new word before children become confident in using it themselves – although the more motivating and meaningful the context, the more likely they are to acquire new vocabulary quickly. It's therefore important to ensure that, as well as the specific 'teaching context' there are other opportunities (e.g. appropriate role-play area, dressing-up clothes, 'small world' toys, games, stories) in which the target words can crop up. Adults can then engage in pole-bridging talk (see page 28) alongside children, and encourage children to pole-bridge, too, or to use the vocabulary naturally in role-play conversation.

Keep a record of words you have targeted, and return to them occasionally. Some children need to keep revisiting familiar words and expressions to gain in language confidence.

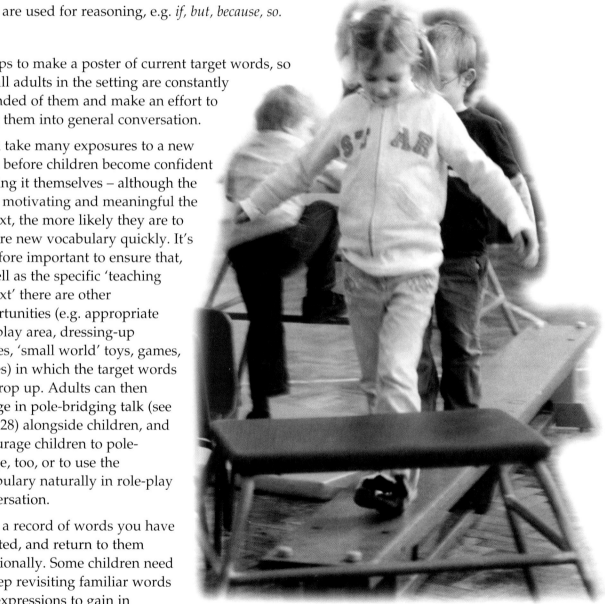

Obstacle courses provide a context for using positional language.

All children misuse words occasionally, but watch out for children who seem excessively confused about vocabulary items. This may indicate an underlying language disorder, and the child should be referred to a speech and language therapist for assessment.

Words that name
What's in the bag?
You will need: an attractive bag and a collection of interesting objects.
Sit the children in a circle with the objects in the middle. Pass the bag around the circle. When you shout 'Stop', the child holding the bag chooses an object from the collection. Encourage them to say, 'I am putting a.... into the bag'. You can vary the objects according to the vocabulary you wish to focus on. When several people have had a turn try to recall who put what into the bag.

Words denoting actions
What am I doing?
Ensure everyone can see everyone else, then perform a simple mime, for example, washing face, eating a banana, brushing teeth. Encourage everyone to copy your mime and name what you're doing. Let the children take turns to start the mime. If they cannot think of actions, use picture cards as a prompt.

How shall we move?
Everyone moves around the room, mingling with each other until you give the signal to stop. You then point to someone and ask them to choose a way for the group to move, for example: jumping, flying, hopping, swooping. When you signal again, everyone stops and another child chooses how to move. You may need to model this process a few times until the children get the hang of it.

Words that describe
Create a 'feely bag' of items of different sizes, shapes, textures and colours.
Children take turns to come out to the front and feel for an item, which they then get to look at, while keeping it hidden from the rest of the class. The child then describes the item for others to guess. Model this process a few times and, if necessary, give children cues (see Report questions in PREPARE chart in Appendix 2).

Words that categorize
Where does it belong?
One of the most effective ways to encourage children to classify objects is to make sure that everything in your setting is well labelled and that there is a place for everything. This provides the children with naturally occurring opportunities to sort and classify when they are getting things out and putting them away again.

Burglar Bill
You will need: a sack and collection of objects from around the classroom.
Tell the children that you found the sack of objects outside the classroom. Invite them to offer their ideas for how it got there! Empty the bag into the middle of the circle, explaining that all the things will need to be sorted out. Hoops are good for sorting into. Model how to choose an item and sort it into the appropriate category, for example: 'I am going to put this spade over here because it belongs with the sand toys.' The children take turns to classify the remaining objects.

Words denoting position
An obstacle course
Set up an obstacle course in the outside area and as children enjoy negotiating their way through, label and describe their actions. Then encourage them to chorus what they're doing as they move, for example: '**under** the chair, **over** the bench, **through** the hoop' and so on.

Rosie's Walk
Read the story of Rosie's Walk, then make your own book featuring positional language. Photograph the children under the table, on top of the climbing frame, going through the gate and so on. When they are the main characters in a book they are avidly interested in it!

Words denoting sequence
Washing-line stories
Peg four pictures, cut-outs or even objects along a washing line, and invent a story in which four events happen in sequence: for example, a character goes for a walk and finds or does things. Model how to tell the story using first, next, then. You could also add in the end, as a way of winding up the story. Ask children to tell their own stories, using their own washing-line items if they wish. Later add in more sequential words, for example, later, finally, after that.

Words used for reasoning
Reasoning words, for example: if, but, because, so, are used naturally whenever language is used to explore, analyse or explain (see pages 34–35).

Repetition and innovation

Children learn to talk by imitating the language of adults, then innovating on these language structures to make them their own. We can help build children's command of vocabulary, sentence structures and questioning techniques by providing language models for them to repeat. This sounds rather dreary, but if transformed into games and role play (see activities opposite) can be great fun. Songs (see Chapter 3: Music, movement and memory) and stories (see Chapter 4: Storytime!) also provide many opportunities for children to imitate the language structures they hear.

Once a language structure is familiar, children can be asked to innovate on it. A powerful vehicle for this is **circle time** (many excellent resources are listed in Recommended resources). A typical circle time activity is to provide a frame, such as '*My favourite place is.... because....*', for each child to complete. If the circle consists of eight children and an adult, by the end of the activity everyone has heard that particular language construction nine times. If the next frame is, '*I don't like going to.... because.... *', that's another nine exposures to the same basic 'reason-giving' structure. Incidentally, don't worry if some children occasionally 'copy' the responses of others – they're still practising language, and gaining in confidence in a social skill.

The language development chart in Appendix 1 indicates the types of language to aim at, depending on children's present stage of development – one simply goes for the next stage up. However, if a topic is sufficiently motivating, they often make surprising progress.

What's this for? is a meaningful context for sentence completion.

Mr Copycat

You will need: a puppet or soft toy to be 'Mr Copycat'.

Introduce Mr Copycat to the children, and explain you want them to repeat whatever he says. You may ask them to do it in chorus to start with, then ask individuals. Mr Copycat (with you as ventriloquist) can then provide sentences that are just at the edge of challenge for the children. Once they've got the idea, vary the activity by asking them to repeat the sentence in a very quiet voice, a loud voice, a robot voice, and so on.

Toy shop

You will need: pictures of toys cut out from a catalogue (provide several of each one to avoid disappointment).

Sit the children in a circle with the pictures in the middle. Explain they are going to pretend they are visiting the toy shop and can choose any toy they'd like. Model the language, for example: '*My name is.... and I am choosing a....*'. Support children who need help by putting in the language for them – with practice they'll soon be joining in. Try the game with colours, fruit or playground equipment. You can vary it to accommodate the vocabulary you wish to teach.

Raps and rhymes

These are a great way of encouraging repetition and innovation, and when language is framed in a rap it also becomes much easier to remember.

What will you play today?

> *What will you play with today* (insert child's name)?
> *What will you play with today?*
> *What will you play with today* (name)?
> *Are you ready to say?*
> Child answers: '*Today, I'm going to play with...*'.

The monkey in town

> *As I was walking through the town, I saw a monkey bending down.*
> *He was bending down and looking at the ground....*
> *and this is what he found.....*

The children then repeat the rhyme and each time they repeat it, they have the monkey find something different.

Pass the parcel

You will need: interesting objects, one of which is duplicated and wrapped in a parcel.

Sit the children in a circle with the objects in the middle. Explain that one of the objects is the same as the one in the parcel. As the parcel is passed around the circle they can guess what's inside. Model the language they need, for example: '*I think that there is a.... inside the parcel*'. Children having difficulties can pick up the object while you model the language for them. As the parcel goes around, the children will hear the language frequently repeated. As children become more skilled they can give a reason for their choice.

Once they've all had a turn, open the parcel and find out what's inside.

Snap shots

Ask the children to bring in a photograph of a member of their family. Sit them in a circle and model how the children are to introduce the person in their photograph, for example: '*This is my.... His/her name is.... I like them because...*', and so on. Children become really engaged with this activity because of the level of emotional engagement.

What's this for?

You will need: a puppet, teddy or soft toy, and a collection of familiar resources.

Explain to the children that your puppet or toy is going to spend the day in your setting, but that he does not understand what all the toys are for and how they are used. Further explain that the children are going to tell him about how each thing is used. Begin by selecting an object and modelling how to give information about it, providing as much information as appropriate for their language level, for example: '*This is called a.... We use it for.... You have to remember...*'. The children then take it in turns to choose an object and, as they pass it around the circle, each child adds to the information.

Developing expressive language

When talking with young children in any context, the use of certain types of expressive language will specifically **PREPARE** them for literacy and learning. We need language to mediate thought when we **P**lan, **R**ecount, **E**xplore, **P**redict, **A**nalyse, **R**eport and **E**xplain, but these are the types of language use which children from 'language-poor' backgrounds often do not use (see PREPARE chart in Appendix 2).

The questions on the chart are not designed to be used as a bombardment! They are simply a guide to the sorts of thinking involved in using language in each of these ways. We must be wary of asking children too many questions, as they may not have the vocabulary with which to answer or, indeed, a clear understanding of underlying concepts, which are often bound up with language. We have to build up this language and understanding gradually by:

- providing models of language use – for example, through pole-bridging talk, or as part of a story

- where possible, providing activities in which these models can be used for repetition and innovation – perhaps through storytelling, drama or role play

- introducing questioning gradually, once we've ensured children are equipped with the vocabulary and experience to answer

- helping children themselves frame questions – again, repetition and innovation can help.

It is helpful to enlarge the **PREPARE** chart and display it as a poster to act as an aide-memoire. In Reception and Year 1, a further poster displaying key question words – *who, what, when, where, why, how and how did you feel?* (accompanied by appropriate symbols) – helps pupils and practitioners ensure that spoken accounts and anecdotes are as explicit as possible.

The EPPE (Effective Provision of Preschool Education) project found that the most important thing we can encourage is 'sustained shared thinking' – this means using talk in ways that *open up children's language*, rather than closed questions (often with one-word answers) that shut it down.

Feely bag activities can be used to encourage explicit language.

Plan

Hold planning sessions directly before periods of child-initiated learning. Talk about what children plan to do and how they'll go about it. Make use of sequencing language (*First, Next, After that*). Encourage children to talk through their plans. Use the 'phone a friend' technique to make this more fun: have plenty of telephones available, and put the children into pairs so that they can tell their plan to each other.

Recount

At the end of a period of child-initiated learning, hold a recount session. Choose a few children to talk about what they did and what happened. (Play games to choose who'll recount next: for example, describe someone, and when the children guess who it is, that person recounts; or spin a bottle and have whoever it stops at, tell what they did.) Stress sequencing language. You can also target recount with children throughout the session, encouraging them to talk about what they've been doing. However, when children are deeply engaged in an activity they sometimes don't want to talk, so be sensitive to their needs.

Explore

Bring in interesting items (or collections of items) for the children to explore, for example: some 'snowstorms'; locks and keys; nuts and bolts; sparkly, costume jewellery. Model exploratory talk: *'I wonder what this is…. I think that bit might be for...'*. When children are exploring, use pole-bridging talk to describe their actions and bring their thoughts to life, *'You're giving that snowstorm a good shake. I wonder what will happen. Where did all the snow come from? I think there must be some water in there or something. The little people are still where they were before. I wonder if that one's the same.'* Leave plenty of gaps for children to join in, or take over the commentary.

Predict

Use stories as a vehicle for prediction (see Chapter 4). As you tell or read a story, stop once in a while to discuss what might happen next. This is a good opportunity for partnered talk. When children have had a minute or so to talk with a partner, invite a few pairs to give their predictions. This can lead you into wondering, *'I wonder why you think that?'* and to linking the prediction to what is already known.

Analyse

Be adventurous with water play. Freeze old keys or 'small world' toys into blocks of ice (use margarine containers). Leave the blocks by the water tray, and join in the amazement when the children discover them, *'What on earth...? What's that ice like? I wonder how it got in there? How can we get it out? Gosh, wasn't that a surprise? I felt really amazed.'* Encourage the children to (a) observe through different senses and consider what they observe, and (b) talk about what they notice, what is happening and how they feel about it. Another time, fill balloons or plastic gloves with water and freeze them.

Report

Create a 'feely bag' (see 'Words that describe' activity on page 31).
To report using other senses, collect a variety of food items (e.g. piece of cheese, tomato ketchup, cocktail sausage, jam, slice of lemon, marshmallow, mashed potato, bearing in mind children's dietary needs, allergies, and so on). Invite children, one by one, behind a screen, and give them an item to hold, feel, sniff and taste. As they do so, ask them to describe it for the others to guess. Model this first, and perhaps help with vocabulary, such as sour, salty, and so on. Ask them to go on and describe visual aspects, such as colour, size and shape, once they have exhausted the descriptive potential of the other senses.

Explain

When interesting phenomena occur, or the group is looking at an item of interest, use 'talking partners' (see page 37) to discuss 'how' and 'why' questions. When children have had a minute or two to talk it over, listen to a few explanations and let the group say which they think most likely.

Social language skills

In Chapter 1: Learning to listen, we looked at two important elements in the social use of language: making eye contact and maintaining attention within conversation. The complementary conversational speaking skills include:

- **engaging the listener's attention** (that is, awareness of and response to one's audience)
- **turn-taking**.

Children need models of these behaviours and opportunities to develop social language skills in context. One of the best contexts is role play, where the adoption of a role allows the child to distance him/herself from the language to some extent, and thus learn from mistakes without personal embarrassment.

All children need frequent opportunities to talk:

- **one-to-one with an adult**, who can model both speaking and listening skills. This is particularly important for children with language delay (see page 26).
- **one-to-one with a peer**, such as a 'talking partner' (see activities opposite and also page 56, Storytime!).
- **in a small group of peers** – for example, in the role-play area.
  The significance of role play cannot be over-estimated. Role-play areas can be skilfully adapted to provide contexts for the sort of language we want children to practise (see page 38).
- **in a small group with an adult** – for example, circle time.
  For very young children and those with language delay, circle time sessions and other group activities are best conducted in groups of about six to eight. As they gain in confidence, the group can grow in size.
- **in a large group**, supervised by an adult.

In the earliest stages, whole-class gatherings will generally be opportunities to listen rather than talk (e.g. early Storytime! activities), but as children grow in confidence, many of the group activities suggested in this chapter can be conducted with the whole class.

The 'talking partner' technique gives every child the opportunity to talk and listen.

Children on the autistic spectrum may have particular difficulties with social language skills. Consult the educational psychological services or local authority special educational needs department for further support. A speech and language therapist can also probably help with social and visual strategies to support the child's access to the curriculum.

2. Time to talk

Pleased to meet you

You will need: a tambourine, a drum or some music.
This game provides an opportunity to model a wide range of social greetings. The children walk around the room, changing direction as they wish until the tambourine is banged or the music stops. They then shake hands with the person nearest to them and greet each other by saying something like, '*Pleased to meet you. How are you today?*' Stop every so often to discuss possible greetings.

Turn-taking object

For children who find it difficult to take turns in conversation, try the circle time technique of using an object – a soft toy or something very special – to denote the speaker. Only the person holding the object is allowed to talk. Karaoke machines can be useful in this respect, as the microphone is usually a highly desirable object, and also helps the rest of the group hear each contribution.

Double circle

This is a way of doing circle time with a larger group, and also introducing 'talking partners'. Invite the children to bring something from home that they would like to talk about. (Bring something of your own, too, so you can model how to talk about an item.) Make two circles of chairs, an inner circle and an outer circle, facing each other. Before the children begin to share, encourage them to think about what they want to say. Then they talk to the person sitting opposite them. If necessary, each pair can have a 'talking object' to determine whose turn it is to talk. On an appointed signal, they swap over and the listener becomes the talker. When they have finished sharing, the inner circle all move round one so that the process can begin again. This enables the children to refine and build on what they want to say.

Talking partners

You can introduce 'talking partners' through the 'double circle', or during conventional circle time ('*Turn to the person on your left and say "Hello…."*.'). Provide many opportunities in this type of structured setting for children to learn how to talk one-to-one with a peer. You could ask them on different occasions to talk about:

- favourite foods, games, animals, television programmes, and so on
- things they like doing; places they like to visit
- a time when they were excited or scared
- things they think they're good at, or find difficult
- one person in their family; where they live
- some work they have done
- what they would choose if they could have any present they wanted.

When they are used to talking to a partner, start to use the technique as a way, during large-group work, of ensuring that every child gets the opportunity to talk about whatever is under discussion: '*Turn to the person on your left and talk about…*'.

Barrier games

Social language to report: Place a familiar object behind a screen and tell the children that you are going to describe this object without actually naming it. Tell them that their job is to listen very carefully and see if they can guess what the object is. When they have seen this modelled a few times encourage them to take on the role of the 'speaker'. Eventually, this can become a partnered task.
Social language to explain: Provide the resources for making or drawing something behind the screen, for instance, a 'Mr Potato Man'. Provide identical equipment on the other side of the screen. The speaker has to create something behind the screen, while explaining to a partner what he/she is doing. The partner, on the other side of the screen, attempts to create exactly the same thing, asking questions when necessary. At the end, they compare their finished results.

Foundations of Literacy   37

Supporting talk during imaginative play

Imaginative play is extremely important for children's all-round development. It also has a crucial role to play in the development of spoken language. Research shows that when children are using the 'pretend self' in imaginative play, they display much greater linguistic competence than at other times. However, if they are to gain maximum rewards from this exciting form of play, it is essential that practitioners think carefully about what is provided.

Providing the environment

Children will play imaginatively just about anywhere in the setting. Whether they are playing in the sand, the water, with 'small world' toys, inside or out, they will be constantly pretending, and in so doing, creating new worlds and confirming familiar ones. Some children's play will be firmly grounded in home and community experiences (socio-dramatic play); others will have begun to enter imagined worlds (thematic-fantasy play). We must provide an appropriate environment and materials for both these types of play:

- a well-equipped **home area**
- **themed areas** where children can engage in transactional play (where goods and services are exchanged for money) – these will vary throughout the year
- **prop boxes** and **dressing-up clothes** that can be used on an ongoing basis to enable children to engage in a wide range of pretend play
- a range of **open-ended materials** to stimulate the imagination so children can use them in their own way
- **story boxes** with props so that children can act out their favourite stories.

The role of the adult

Before setting up any imaginative play area, give careful consideration to the following questions:

- Is what we are intending within the children's experience, and if not, what can we do about it? For instance, we could take them on a visit, read stories, watch videos and look at pictures or model the role play ourselves. Once children have seen adults model the process they will be much more confident about doing it themselves. If necessary, sit the children down in front of the role-play area and let them watch the adults role-playing.
- Can we involve the children in planning and setting up the imaginative play area? If we can, it will be a much more important place for them.
- Do we have a programme for observing children in the imaginative play area so that we are aware of what they are talking about and what vocabulary they are using? Only by doing this can we add new materials, make suggestions and provide further experiences that will develop their language yet further.
- Are we providing a balance of adult-initiated and child-initiated activities?
- Have we given enough consideration to how we will interact with children in the imaginative play area?
- Have we made some time each day to join the children in the role-play area?
- Do we give children positive (and differentiated) feedback on their activities?

If you are unfortunate enough to be working with restricted space, make the best possible use of story boxes, prop boxes and the outside area (see Recommended resources – using story boxes and builder's trays).

Chapter Three

Music, movement and **memory**

Music, movement and memory

Music seems to be a natural form of communication with young children. It provides a playful, emotionally satisfying context for all sorts of learning, a context that is associated with relaxation and fun. Since time immemorial, parents have sung nursery rhymes, played clapping games and taught action songs to entertain their children, and teachers used to continue that tradition in school. Unfortunately, in today's society, home entertainment is more likely to come in visual form, and the old songs and chants are often forgotten. In school, time for music and song has often been eroded by the demands of the national curriculum and, of course, the National Literacy and Numeracy strategies.

Music, especially song, is an obvious way of developing all the important listening skills described in Chapter 1. Since most musical activities are performed in a group, they are also ideal for developing social skills of collaboration, including turn-taking and learning to sing in time with the rest of the group (see Chapter 2). Phonemic awareness, which underpins phonics, seems to depend to a large extent on the appreciation of rhythm, auditory discrimination and memory (see Chapter 6), while musical activities – from simple clapping games, through marching, action songs and dances – also help children develop gross and fine motor control, hand-eye co-ordination and physical confidence – all essential for handwriting (see Chapter 7).

Given the extent to which musical experience in the early years appears to contribute to children's ability to read and write, we should ensure that it is a valued part of our daily practice throughout the Foundation Stage.

Development of steady beat, rhythm and rhyme

Research from High/Scope in the USA (see Further reading) suggests that a young child's ability to **keep a steady beat** is one of the best indicators of later academic success. This will come as no surprise to early years practitioners, as young children who are naturally able to sing and keep time often have a maturity and language competence beyond that of their peers. In the earliest stages, the ability to maintain steady beat may well aid the development of speech, as a sense of timing underlies our ability to pick up the patterns of spoken phrases and sentences. As soon as possible, therefore, we should provide activities to help children feel the strong 'pulse' or beat in speech and in music.

In terms of literacy, one of the key stages of phonological awareness (outlined on page 78) is the ability to discriminate syllables – the 'beats' within a word. Appreciation of rhythm also leads children to recognize rhyming patterns, critical for the learning of phonics. Once they have acquired this level of phonological awareness, children seem to delight in it, and there is a strong playground culture of clapping, skipping and 'dipping' rhymes, which exploit rhythm, nonsense syllables and rhymes (e.g. 'Ee-ny, mee-ny, mi-ny, mo; Catch a ti-ger by the toe; If he holl-ers, let him go; Ee-ny, mee-ny, mi-ny, mo; I say you are IT!').

For reading and writing, children must also be sensitive to the rhythms and patterns of **written language**, which is more complex and organized than the language of spontaneous speech. Musical activities lay the foundations for sensitivity to the 'tunes and cadences' of written phrases, sentences and paragraphs – what Robert Louis Stevenson called 'the chime of fine words, and the stately march of the period'. It's possible that, at a later stage of education, understanding of punctuation and the ability to read with expression have their roots in enjoyable early rhythm-based activities.

When playing **chopsticks** ensure children know it is a music game. At home or in a restaurant, such behaviour with chopsticks would be the height of bad manners!

Keep the beat

Sit the children in a circle and put on some music that has a strong beat. Encourage the children to:

- ✎ while sitting down, pat the beat on their knees using both hands
- ✎ while sitting down, pat the beat alternating hands
- ✎ while sitting down, stamp the beat using feet alternately
- ✎ walk or march to the beat while standing in one place
- ✎ walk or march to the beat in a forwards, backwards or sideways direction.

Chopsticks

You will need: some paper plates and some chopsticks.

- ✎ Give out the paper plates and, using the chopsticks, play a simple sequence of sounds to a steady beat on the reverse side of the plates. For example, you could use the sticks to hit the floor, plate, floor, plate, floor, plate, and so on.
- ✎ As the children gain in confidence and skill make the sequence more complicated – for example, floor, plate, knock your sticks together, plate, floor, plate, sticks together, plate, and so on. Give hands-on guidance to children experiencing difficulty. This will enable them to 'feel' the beat.
- ✎ When children become proficient, allow them to take the lead.
- ✎ Try this activity using inexpensive plastic, wastepaper baskets turned upside down.

Rap it out

Rapping allows children to explore the musicality of language. Begin by devising simple raps and proceed to more difficult ones like the following:

My gran's cupboard
My gran has a cupboard under the stairs,
And every time I look in there,
I see some things that make me shout,
Some things that make my eyes pop out,
I see a monster, right there,
Right there under the stairs!

(The children can generate further ideas for what might be under the stairs and then rap a sequence of things. This will really develop the auditory memory!)

Who is knocking at my door?
Ten dirty dogs came knocking at my door,
Rat-a-tat, rat-a-tat, knocking at my door,
Ten dirty dogs came knocking at my door,
Till I said, 'dirty dogs DON'T DO IT ANY MORE'
So they didn't, but then….

(Repeat the rhyme substituting, for example, mucky monkeys, grubby gorillas, cool cats, slithering snakes, and so on.)

Beat out a name

- ✎ Tell the children you're going to clap out a forename of a child, for them to guess who it is. Clap the number of syllables in the longest names (e.g. Victoria, Alexander). When they answer correctly, ask the owners out beside you, pronouncing their names syllabically (Vic-tor-i-a).
- ✎ Then clap a syllable for the shortest names (e.g. Jade, Sam), and again, when children recognize their names, bring those owners out, too. Clap any remaining names until everyone is with you.
- ✎ When children are familiar with the idea of clapping their names, you can use it in day-to-day organization, for example for lining up ('*If I clap your name, stand up now. Lovely – you can go and line up. Is there anyone else? Listen!*'), until gradually everyone is hearing the beats in words.

Further suggestions for activities (and plenty of fun songs and raps) can be found in Ros's Rap Packs, and other steady beat materials (Lawrence Education).

Articulation and song

We did not comment on articulation skills in Chapter 2, despite their importance in the development of spoken language, because of constraints of space. However, a chart describing the normal development of articulation is given in Appendix 1, and practitioners should keep an ear on children's speech to ensure this is developing appropriately.* Singing helps refine young children's articulatory skills in an enjoyable way, and songs are a good way of introducing or reinforcing new vocabulary. Singing also develops control of vocal expression, introducing a range of pitches, volumes and subtleties.

The choice of songs is important. Children today sometimes learn to sing along with pop songs at home but these have short shelf lives, and are not shared across the generations (especially with older practitioners!) in the same way as traditional songs. If children enjoy singing them, it's fine to include them in your repertoire, but try also to include:

- nursery rhymes and chants, which are highly rhythmic, with plenty of rhyme and alliteration, and seem to be particularly suitable in terms of preparation for phonics (see Chapter 6)

- action songs, which also engage kinesthetic memory, and can be useful for developing motor skills, hand-eye co-ordination and, in the case of finger-rhymes, the muscles required for adequate pencil grip (see Chapter 7)

- songs with choruses for joining in, but particularly those that require turn-taking, or give opportunities for different children to sing variations on a familiar verse structure.

Action songs encourage kinesthetic as well as auditory memory.

*Articulation, like all language skills, depends upon a child's hearing ability, and upon adequate exposure to interactive spoken language. If, despite these conditions being met, articulation is poor and a child does not seem able to copy your 'correct models' of pronunciation, refer him or her to a speech and language therapist for assessment. Take great care never to inhibit children's speech by making them self-conscious about problems with articulation.

Singing with young children

First and foremost, have fun! Singing should be an enjoyable activity – don't worry about the quality of the sound produced as young children are still 'finding their voice'. Young children have a limited vocal range so avoid songs that are outside this range, as they'll simply be unable to join in. If you are unsure about this range be aware of the type of tunes they sing spontaneously while playing! Musical accompaniment isn't necessary – indeed, music from an instrument often drowns out the children's singing and makes it difficult for them to hear their own voices. However, they will need you to sing with them, to teach them the tune and words. Don't worry if you feel your voice is not very good – the children will not judge you. You are their model and if you sing with confidence, so will they. Commercially produced tapes and CDs are also useful as they help you maintain the beat, but make sure they are pitched appropriately within the children's vocal range.

A daily sing-song

A short singing session each day is much better than a long session once a week. First thing in the morning is a very good time for a sing-along session, as it tunes the children into the day (and into speaking and listening in a group) in a pleasant way, and singing together establishes a feeling of cohesion in the class. Get children to stand up when singing as this helps them to breathe more easily and produce a better sound – also they will almost certainly want to move as they sing, whether it's an action song or not! Always begin a session with a well-known and well-loved song. Introduce new songs gradually.

Songs throughout the day

Wherever possible, integrate more songs into the daily routine of the setting, for example:

- sing the register
- use a song to introduce a regular event such as 'Storytime' – when they hear you start the song, or play the tune on a CD, everyone gradually joins in and makes their way to the story corner. This rap, by music specialist Linda Caroe, works a treat: '1, 2, 3, 4, Come and sit down on the floor; 5, 6, 7, 8, Hurry up and don't be late; 1, 2, 3, 4, Is your bottom on the floor? 5, 6, 7, 8, Are you sitting really straight?'
- make up a tidy-up song (as generations of workers have discovered, chores become much easier if accompanied by a song). Linda Caroe's tidy-up song goes to the tune of *The Farmer's in his Den*: 'It's time to tidy up, it's time to tidy up. Ee, i, addio, it's time to tidy up. We're tidying the paints, etc. We're tidying the chairs, etc...'.
- singing a special 'goodbye song' is a calm and pleasant way to end the day.

Which songs?

When they come into an early years setting, many children may already have built up a repertoire of favourite songs. Ask them what they would like to sing and encourage them to teach their favourite songs to each other. There are many tapes and CDs of nursery rhymes and songs, and the publishers A & C Black produce a wide variety of songbooks. Look out particularly for:

- traditional action songs, for example: *There Was A Princess Long Ago*; *In A Cottage In A Wood*; *Wind The Bobbin Up*; *Incy Wincy Spider*; *If You're Happy And You Know It Clap Your Hands*; *The Farmer's In His Den*
- traditional songs that can be acted out or turned into action rhymes, for example: *Row, Row, Row Your Boat*; *Polly Put The Kettle On*; *Twinkle, Twinkle Little Star*; *She'll Be Coming Round The Mountain When She Comes*; *Strawberry Fair*; *Old Uncle Tom Cobleigh*
- number and cumulative songs which, when familiar, can be adapted to give different children (or groups) a short piece each to sing, with the whole group singing the main chorus, for example: *Old MacDonald Had A Farm*; *There Were Ten In The Bed*; *Ten Green Bottles*; *Five Little Speckled Frogs*; *One Man Went To Mow*; *One, Two, Three, Four, Five, Once I Caught a Fish Alive*; *Green Grow The Rushes-O!* (as children's voices extend their range).

Once children know a song well, encourage them to be innovative by playing with and changing some of the words and ideas. For example, Old MacDonald could have a shop instead of a farm. Everyone could go round the supermarket instead of the Mulberry Bush.

Music and auditory memory

As discussed in Chapter 1, auditory memory – the ability to recall sequences of sound – is extremely important for learning, and especially for literacy learning. All musical activities involve remembering sequences of sound, and the memorization is made easier by the elements of melody, rhythm and repetition. Indeed, if you want someone to remember something, put it to music – as successful advertising demonstrates! Hence the success of songs for counting, learning the alphabet, days of the week, and so on.

Action songs and rhymes, marching, clapping chants and simple dances also involve the kinesthetic learning channel, offering support for children who need extra help in developing auditory memory. Even those children who aren't yet ready to join in are still able to participate by making the movements and building up a predictive sequence in the brain. And, of course, these activities can be repeated time and again, without ever boring the children.

'Row, row, row the boat...'

For activities involving a dynamic combination of music or rhythm and movement, children need space – preferably much more space than is available in the average classroom. It's therefore essential that, somehow, regular provision is also made for these activities in open areas – indoors in a hall, gym or other large space, or outdoors in the play area, a park or sports field.

The following examples illustrate how a single action rhyme or song can be useful in a variety of ways. Teach the rhyme for fun, and as a way of remembering the days of the week, colours, and so on. Later, when alerting children to the long vowel sounds, revisit the familiar rhyme and ask them to listen for, then exaggerate the pronunciation of, the particular phoneme each time it occurs.

Days of the week (and the long 'ay' sound)

Monday, a plane to fly far away,
Tuesday, a scooter to go out to play,
Wednesday, a ship, we're sailing to Spain,
Thursday, chuff chuff, we're off on the train!
Friday, a rocket to blast into space,
Saturday, we're in a car in a race,
Sunday, we sit and we play and we talk,
Then when we're ready, we'll go for a walk!

Devise suitable actions for each vehicle…. end up with everyone walking round.

Parts of the body (and the long 'ee' sound)

Easy peasy, lemon squeezy
Stretch your arms and bend your kneezy!

Easy peasy, lemon squeezy
Rub your tum and bend your kneezy!

Use the following to make up more verses: *Tap your head…. , clap your hands…. , touch your nose…. , cross your legs....* (which, if you do it when bending your knees, will mean you all fall over!).

Colours and directions (and the long 'igh' sound)

I'm a kite, a bright red kite,
I fly to the left, I fly to the right,
I start off low, I fly up high,
See me flying in the sky.

The tune is adapted from *Twinkle, Twinkle Little Star* (basically the first two lines repeated). Make kite shapes for the children to colour. Each child holds up a kite of a different colour, while singing and acting out one verse of the song.

Quick and slow (and the long 'oa' sound)

Row, row, row the boat,
Slow as slow can be,
Row, row, row the boat,
Slowly over the sea.

Row, row, row the boat,
Quick as quick can be,
Row, row, row the boat,
Quickly over the sea.

Sing to the original tune, making rowing actions. Vary the speed appropriately.

A counting rhyme (and the long 'oo' sound)

Oo oo dippity doo, how many tigers in the zoo?
I can count quite a few (count them, all together)
But there's only one kangaroo.
(boo hoo)

Put children in groups of varying numbers and give each group an animal identity, such as monkeys, penguins, pandas, parrots and lions. An adult can be the lonely kangaroo, saying 'boo hoo' at the end of each verse.

Left–right brain interaction

Doing the *Hokey Cokey* (*'You put your left arm in...'*) and marching with *The Grand Old Duke of York* (*'left, right, left, right'*) has taught many generations of children two important words – and the underlying concepts – needed to help develop L→R directionality in reading and writing.

However, there's much more to left and right than that. Reading and writing are highly complex tasks, involving the integration of mental activity in both the left and right hemispheres of the brain. For instance, in order to read with understanding, a child must be able to combine:

- phonic decoding (the sort of small, sequential, analytic processing task associated with the left brain)

- overall comprehension of the text (the type of holistic understanding associated with the right brain).

Physical activity that involves controlled and integrated movement of both sides of the body helps children develop connections between the two hemispheres of the brain required for this sort of 'balanced' mental activity. The *Hokey Cokey*, marching games, action songs, skipping and dancing fulfil all these requirements, as well as developing children's motor control and hand-eye co-ordination in preparation for the physical skills of handwriting (see Chapter 7).

Sadly, there has been little work to date on the significance of music in language and literacy development. Current brain-based research indicates that music and language involve activity in many of the same parts of the brain, although music seems to be centred in the right hemisphere and language in the left. We suspect there is a 'missing link' here that, if we could fathom it, might be of great help to those children for whom, at present, literacy skills do not come easily.

Simple 'crossed hands' dances are a good starting point for movement to music.

All sorts of dance

- ✎ Provide a music area with plenty of music with a strong beat. Teach the children how to operate the CD player and encourage them to dance, dance, dance!

- ✎ Show children how to do a simple circle dance. If they have trouble staying together, provide a large piece of covered elastic that they can hold on to. If you don't want to make your own, you can get one from JABADAO (see Recommended resources).

- ✎ If any parents are line-dancers, ask them to bring in some music and teach the children some of the simplest moves.

Left right, left right!

March, march and march, as you move from one place to another. Have a marching band and lead children in procession around the outside area. Make ankle bands by sewing some bells onto some elastic and let the children wear them as they 'march'. This way, they will hear and feel the regular beat as they move. Provide regimental marching tunes for them to march to, and other marching music – pretend they're soldiers or cheerleaders, whichever they prefer!

Brain Gym®

There are many Brain Gym® activities to encourage cross-over actions. For example, the 'cross crawl' involves standing up and alternately raising the left knee to touch the right elbow and the right knee to touch the left elbow. Any such activity is easier if set to music.

Passing games

- ✎ Sit the children in a circle and give out three or four beanbags. As you sing, pass the beanbags around the circle, encouraging the children to pass them on the 'beat'.

- ✎ Use cuddly toys, and as you sing pass the toys around the circle. Adapt a well-known song as a passing song, for example: '*Here we go passing the ted around, ted around, ted around*' (instead of going round the *Mulberry Bush*).

- ✎ Pass a tambourine around the circle. As each child receives the tambourine, they bang it a specified number of times.

Bim, bam, boom!

Provide plenty of opportunities for drumming. If you don't have conventional drums use old paint tins, saucepans, wastepaper bins, dustbins, etc. Tie off the ends of washing-up mops and use as beaters.

Also important for encouraging cross-over movements:

- ✎ Ensure that children have ongoing, daily access to a well-equipped outside area where they can engage in cross-lateral movement naturally as they play.

- ✎ Facilitate opportunities for crawling by providing plenty of low tunnels. If you don't have any, open up the ends of cardboard boxes and join them together with parcel tape. Provide boxes and tape for the children to construct their own tunnels!

- ✎ Provide plenty of opportunities for children to walk across low balance bars and construct bridges for them to cross.

A musical setting

Early years practitioners have always recognized the crucial importance of music in the overall development of the child, but now that research into brain development is confirming what we have always intuitively known, it's even more important to pay serious attention to the quality of our provision for music. As well as adult-initiated musical activities, there should be plenty of opportunities for children to expand their interest, involvement and skills through their own child-initiated music and song.

Listening to and making music

- Provide a listening centre where children can go to listen to a range of music from a variety of different cultures.

- Encourage children to develop their critical response and express their opinions with regard to which pieces of music and which songs they most like, and why.

- Take advantage of opportunities for the children to hear adults and older children singing and playing instruments.

- Provide high quality music areas (both inside and out if possible), where children can go to explore sound and handle instruments that can be beaten, shaken, blown or strummed. When children are working with sound makers, offer sensitive support and encouragement, asking questions that will steer them into offering their ideas about how the instruments might be used.

- Ensure children are taught how to care for the resources.

- Collect objects and materials (e.g. recycled household objects and packaging), which the children can use to make musical instruments.

Songs and rhymes

- Try to ensure a balance between the adult- and child-initiated singing. For example, once you have taught the children a song, provide a tape recorder so that they can practise and refine it during periods of child-initiated learning.

- Invite children to choose which songs they would most like to sing, or rhymes to recite.

- Encourage children to have fun with language by making up their own songs, raps and jingles.

- When adults have modelled the possibilities, allow the children to take the lead, and build on what they have seen and heard to make it their own.

Musical performance

- Provide a performance area where children can go to perform musical pieces, movement sequences and dances – this could easily be outside. Look for something to value in every effort. A karaoke machine can make this a very popular activity.

- Provide a range of objects and fabrics, such as scarves, ribbon, sticks, beanbags, lengths of material and so on, so that children can develop movement ideas for moving to music.

- Encourage and help children to tape their own songs and musical compositions.

- Occasionally, video musical or dance performances for children to watch themselves later.

Chapter Four

Storytime**!**

Storytime!

In the past, to share in a story, children had to listen. Whether gathered around a storyteller, drinking in the repetitive, patterned language of the oral tradition, or listening to a storybook read aloud, children engaged with the story by ear. Today, however, almost half the nation's 4 year olds have a television in their bedrooms. For many, listening to a story is a thing of the past.

Stories on screen are mostly visual – viewers *watch* the characters and the setting, following the plot with their eyes. For many contemporary children, a story has no 'voice' or narrative thread – just fragmented dialogue, sound effects and background music. Indeed, they are often even unaware that the story has a beginning, middle and end – they experience it as a conceptual whole.

These children may have difficulty learning to read. You might teach them phonics and sight words, and demonstrate how to trawl through big books, but if the language of text is unfamiliar, the 'shape' of stories unknown and their ears untrained to narrative, they'll find it hard to make sense of what you're doing. At a later stage, when asked to write a story, they'll be at a loss, because stories on screen do not stimulate the imagination. Neither do they model the use of words to tell a tale, describe a setting or bring characters to life.

Before formal literacy begins, we must first immerse children in 'story language' by replicating the activities of old: story-telling and reading aloud.

Story-telling: developing listening skills

Story-telling develops all aspects of listening. The adult storyteller, unhampered by a book, can make eye contact with the children, modelling how to use facial and vocal expression, gesture and body language, to maintain their attention. The rhythmic, repetitive, patterned language of the oral tradition – along, hopefully, with plenty of audience participation – develop attention span and auditory memory. We therefore recommend that, at any time, you have a repertoire of at least four or five stories, to be told and retold, at least one each day.

To draw children under the spell of a story you can also use puppets, pictures and props. These, of course, also help the storyteller. For instance, if your story involves finding a number of items during a walk in the forest, you can have the items on your knee in a bag, ready to produce with a flourish. Or you can create a story map, with pictures of the main events, which acts as a prompt to you and an illustration for the audience. Each performance should also highlight the key elements of a story (beginning, middle and end; and well-defined characters and settings).

Story-telling is a powerful way to develop children's speaking and listening skills, and anybody can do it! You don't have to be an extrovert, you don't need any special qualifications and it doesn't matter if you make a mistake -– the children will revel in your blunders and enjoy putting you right!

However, when you're first getting started it may help to rehearse. If you record your story on tape – using plenty of key phrases and repetition – and listen to it several times (perhaps in the car driving to and from work, joining in as it becomes more familiar), you will soon commit it to memory.

Some traditional stories for telling:

The Gingerbread Man	*Goldilocks and the Three Bears*	*Red Riding Hood*
Three Billy Goats Gruff	*Jack and the Beanstalk*	*The Little Red Hen*
Three Little Pigs	*The Enormous Turnip*	*Chicken Licken*

These tales demonstrate the strengths of a good story – well-developed characters (not too many and not too complex), repetition, build-up of the plot, good overcoming evil and a happy ending. However, the best stories are those you make up yourself, to fit the needs of the children you work with (see activities opposite).

Stories can be illustrated with picture cards along a washing line.

Telling children stories

Soft toy stories

Soft toys make an excellent focus for story-telling because they engage children's emotions. Select a character that appeals to you, because this helps you believe in your character and tell your story well – if you don't believe in it, your listeners won't! Find a special bag from which to produce the toy when he makes his first appearance as this heightens the excitement. Tell the children that you have someone special that wants to meet them, then slowly reveal the toy. Floppy, soft toys are best as they are easy to manipulate. Sit the toy on your hand and use your other hand to move the head as you tell your story about the character (practise in front of a mirror – you'll be amazed at the range of expressions you can achieve).

Puppet stories

All that has been said about soft toys also applies to puppets. Once you have one or two popular characters, your stories can go on and on. You can create your own soap opera, and the more the children hear about your characters, the more they will want to hear!

Make the most of your camera

Take your puppets and toys out into the community and the wider world and photograph them in different settings – people might stare, but who cares! Such photographs create the basis for many exciting stories.

Pictures and artefacts

You can also illustrate a story with picture cards, postcards or pictures from old calendars. A series of pictures can really spark the imagination. You can peg them along a washing line as the story progresses, to help children remember the sequence of events. Artefacts can be even more effective, as children can handle them as you tell the story. Start making a collection of interesting objects and let your imagination run wild!

Story sacks

These take time to put together, but if everyone contributes and the work is shared you can soon build up a collection (see *Storysacks* in Recommended resources). Or, if you prefer, you can buy ready-made ones to go with picture books.

Plots

When it comes to a plot, keep it simple. Two important considerations are:

- ✎ A 'match of meaning' – in other words, whatever is happening to your character must match the children's experience in some way; they must be able to relate to it. That way, they will listen with real absorption.
- ✎ Make it memorable, so you (or a child) can tell it again – repetition is helpful here. For example, your character(s) could go on a walk and find/do numerous things, or meet various people; or there could be a series of ways of solving a problem (*First, Next, In the end*).

When planning your story, you may find this list of universal themes useful:

Getting lost or losing something	Getting into trouble
Finding (an) interesting item(s)	Feeling jealous
Helping someone	Being bullied/picked on
Feeling afraid	Winning and losing
Split loyalties	Mistaken identity
Disappointment	Accidents
Making choices/moral conflict	Not thinking ahead
Disregarding/breaking rules	Dishonesty
Acting bravely; self-sacrifice	Taking revenge
Being surprised	Getting locked in/trapped
Endeavour	Journeys and quests

Story-telling: developing speaking skills

Story-telling is a wonderful way of increasing children's vocabulary, sentence structure and confidence. If you model story-telling and also work with the children, crafting stories together (see activities opposite), they will soon become confident and adventurous storytellers themselves. Once individuals are ready to tell their own stories, a storyteller's chair or hat makes the experience really special. For many children, this will be the first opportunity to speak uninterrupted for any length of time – a great confidence boost.

From the point of view of literacy development, story-telling has a further advantage for children. It familiarizes them with 'story grammar' – the key ingredients and 'shape' of a story. Listening to lots of stories and making up their own means that, when they eventually come to write stories, they won't struggle to invent characters, settings and plots.

And story-telling does not have to mean fiction. We all have real-life stories to tell, and children can be encouraged to tell stories about themselves – holiday adventures, anecdotes about 'when they were little' or accounts of events connected to a topic under study. Story-telling can become a regular feature of partnered work: *'Tell your story to your partner….'*, after which a few stories can be shared with the whole class.

Learning stories by heart

Listening to adults telling stories can lead to another type of spoken language: recitation. For children unfamiliar with stories, this can be deeply satisfying. It also develops auditory memory and familiarizes children with key sentence constructions. This is why we recommend the repeated retelling of some favourite stories. After a few listening sessions, most children pick up and can be encouraged to join in with sections of the story. You can encourage this by devising simple actions to accompany key words and phrases, bringing in the added benefit of kinesthetic memory, and drawing a simple story map.

A story-telling chair makes the experience of telling a story very special.

Once a story is familiar, you can sit back, letting the children take over completely. If they lose the thread, you can provide a prompt (the next phrase, an action, or pointing to the story map). To begin with, recitation will be a choral activity – with some children carrying the others along – but eventually you can encourage individuals to tell the story verbatim, either one-to-one or in a small group. Alternatively, children can tell a story to a talking partner, who takes on the role of the adult, prompting where necessary. By building a store of characters, plots and story-language in this way, children will find it easier to create their own stories, in role play, story-telling sessions and, in later years, when they come to write.

> **Watch out for children who do not join in, and provide more one-to-one interaction (see page 26) or perhaps opportunities to retell favourite stories in a group of two or three.**

Children telling stories

Magic box

For this activity, you will need the co-operation of parents.
Explain to the children that they will take it in turns to take the magic box home and place it on the windowsill in their bedroom. When they wake up in the morning there will be something for them in the magic box – explain to parents that this need only be a small token. The following morning the child brings the box back to school and tells everyone about what they have found in the box.

The journey

You will need: some play people, animal figures, pictures from magazines depicting settings, vehicles and activities, and a box of miscellaneous artefacts.
Sit the children in a circle with the resources in containers in the middle: characters, settings, vehicles, activities and objects. Explain that you are going to make up a story about some friends who go on a journey. Pass an object around the circle, explaining that whoever has the object when you give the signal (this can be a bell, handclap, etc), gets to choose a character. Encourage the child who selects the character to set the scene, for example: '*Once upon a time, there was a ....*'. Continue to pass the object around until the children have chosen and added to the spoken story: another character; a place where they went; a vehicle for them to travel in and an activity that they took part in. Finally, on the way home, they can find something (child chooses from the box of mixed artefacts). Model how the story might end, and once they have seen you do this a few times they will soon begin to do it for themselves.

Story bag

You will need: an attractive bag and some interesting and unusual artefacts, such as an old key, magnifying glass, map, binoculars, a crystal or precious stone.
Tell the children that you are going to make up a story about the day they went on a very unusual school trip. Ask for suggestions for where the story may be set and how it might start. Invite children to take turns drawing an object out of the bag, and weaving a story about what happened when each item was found. If there are several suggestions, have them consider which would be most appropriate, and if they become stuck, offer a few suggestions of your own.

Our special character

One of the best ways to generate stories is to create your own character, arising from the children's interests. You could use a toy (a lonely teddy?) or even make a full-size model (some Scottish children made 'Mr Togs the Tailor' and he lived in a tailor's shop in their classroom for half a year!). The children can be involved in deciding: the character's name, where s/he lives (can you make this home as a role-play area?) and who s/he lives with; the character's personality and what s/he likes doing. Once their characters have become established, you can go on to create situations to which the children can make a response, and in so doing, you may find the universal themes on page 55 helpful. Some useful starting points for children's stories are:

- taking your character in covered in plasters or bandaged up – '*What happened?*'
- having your character be upset because a favourite toy has been broken
- maybe your character is frightened because s/he has to go to the dentist
- having the character 'disappear' – 'Where's s/he gone?' (S/he could leave a note or send a postcard.)

The children could also take it in turns to take the character home for the weekend and then tell the story of what happened during that time.

Many ideas for developing language by learning stories by heart can be found in Pie Corbett's *The Bumper Book of Story Telling into Writing at Key Stage 1* (Clown Publishing, 2006).

Reading aloud – five a day!

Some children are lucky enough to learn to read 'naturally' – a parent or carer sits and shares favourite books time after time with the child joining in, until he or she can 'read along' (which is initially just reciting). Gradually, through years of this sort of enjoyable interaction, the child begins to recognize certain words and to associate letters with sounds. We can replicate this process by reading children **at least five books** every day, repeatedly returning to favourites, until pupils 'read along'. In a group, less able children are often supported in this by watching their peers, and we can help the learning process by sometimes setting the words to music or adding actions.

'Five a day' sessions should be at regular times, and should not take long – perhaps ten to fifteen minutes at the start of the day, after break or before home time. Short picture books with lots of repetition (e.g. *Where's Spot?*, *Farmer Duck*, *Handa's Surprise*) and rhyme and rhythm (e.g. *This is the Bear*, *We're Going on a Bear Hunt*) are ideal, and once children are familiar with them, will not take long to read. New books should be introduced gradually into the 'five a day' routine, perhaps one or two new titles per week. When you introduce a new book you may want to spend some time talking about it, but thereafter **don't interrupt the story with talk**. Just read the book for fun and let it speak for itself! With frequent rereadings, children should be able to learn by heart at least ten story books a term, so eventually you can sit back, and let the group – or individual children – take the lead and 'read' the book.

'Five a day' develops many of the same skills as 'story-telling' (see page 54) – especially auditory memory – but with an important bonus: children begin to internalize the patterns of written language. Familiarity with written sentence structures is, of course, essential before children can use grammatical cues to predict words in text, an important skill for reading. By Reception, in the early rereadings of stories, you can start to develop children's prediction skills orally by occasionally stopping as you read, and letting them fill in the missing word – but don't overdo this. The key element in reading aloud should **always** be pleasure: don't ever let it turn into a chore.

Read the book, without interruptions, and let it speak for itself.

50 books for reading aloud

The most important factor in selecting a book to read aloud is that you enjoy reading it yourself. The following list is composed of tried and tested children's favourites:

Alfie Gets In First Shirley Hughes (Red Fox)
Amazing Grace Mary Hoffman (Frances Lincoln)
Angry Arthur Hiawyn Oram and Satsoshi Kitamura (Red Fox)
Bear Snores On Karma Wilson and June Chapman (Simon and Schuster)
Billy's Sunflower Nicola Moon (Little Hippo)
Brown Bear, Brown Bear, What Do You See? Bill Martin Jnr and Eric Carle (Puffin)
Danny's Duck June Crebbin (Walker Books)
Dear Zoo Rod Campbell (Puffin)
Dig Dig Digging Margaret Mayo (Orchard Books)
Doctor Dog Babette Cole (Red Fox)
Dogger Shirley Hughes (Picture Lions)
Doing the Animal Bop Jan Ormerod and Lindsey Gardiner (Oxford)
Duck in the Truck Jez Alborough (Collins)
Each Peach Pear Plum Janet and Allan Ahlberg (Puffin)
Elmer David McKee (Red Fox)
Farmer Duck Martin Waddell (Walker)
Funnybones Janet and Allan Ahlberg (Puffin)
Gorilla Anthony Browne (Red Fox)
Hairy Maclary from Donaldson's Dairy Lynley Dodd (Puffin)
Handa's Surprise Eileen Browne (Walker)
Is It Bedtime Wibbly Pig? Mick Inkpen (Hodder)
Little Rabbit Foo Foo Michael Rosen and Arthur Robbins (Walker)
Mr Gumpy's Outing John Burningham (Red Fox)
Mr Magnolia Quentin Blake (Red Fox)
No Matter What Debi Gliori (Bloomsbury)
Not Now Bernard David McKee (Red Fox)
One Snowy Night Nick Butterworth (Collins)
Owl Babies Martin Waddell (Walker)
Pants Giles Andreae and Nick Sharratt (Picture Corgi)
Pass the Jam Jim Kaye Umansky and Margaret Chamberlain (Red Fox)
Peace at Last Jill Murphy (Macmillan)
Pumpkin Soup Helen Cooper (Picture Corgi)
Rosie's Walk Pat Hutchinson (Red Fox)
So Much Trish Cooke (Walker Books)
Solo Paul Geraghty (Hutchinson)
That's Not My Puppy Fiona Watt (Usbourne)
The Bear Under the Stairs Helen Cooper (Corgi)
The Elephant and the Bad Baby Elfrida Vipont and Raymond Briggs (Puffin)
The Gingerbread Boy Ian Beck (Oxford University Press)
The Gruffalo Julia Donaldson and Alex Scheffler (Macmillan Children's Books)
The Owl Who Was Afraid of the Dark Jill Tomlinson (Egmont)
The Tiger Who Came to Tea Judith Kerr (Collins)
The Time It Took Tom Nick Sharratt (Scholastic)
The Very Hungry Caterpillar Eric Carle (Puffin)
There Was An Old Lady Who Swallowed a Fly Pam Adams (Child's Play)
This is the Bear Sarah Hayes and Helen Craig (Walker)
We're Going on a Bear Hunt Michael Rosen and Helen Oxenbury (Walker)
Where the Wild Things Are Maurice Sendak (Red Fox)
Where's My Teddy? Jez Alborough (Walker)
Where's Spot? Eric Hill (Puffin)

Developing imaginative engagement

Stories, told or read, provide the basis for many imaginative activities – all of which develop spoken language skills and children's ability to engage with stories, and with each other.

- **Drama**: help the children turn the story into a play, taking turns to play the parts of the characters (perhaps, if they know the story by heart, the rest of the group could act as choral narrators). In the early stages, this may need modelling (see page 38). Plays may be totally informal, or children can help make costumes, props and scenery, and turn it into a full-scale performance.

- **Role play**: this will happen naturally, but you can encourage it by providing the props and dressing-up clothes to turn the role-play area into the three bears' house, the giant's castle, and so on. Of course, role play doesn't need to happen in the 'corner' – a few carefully arranged chairs or boxes can become the *Train Ride,* any room can be transformed into the landscape of the *Bear Hunt,* and so on.

- **Retelling**: story maps, time lines, fuzzy felt characters, masks, puppets, soft toys, and so on, all encourage children to retell stories. Pictures of old copies of a favourite book can be cut out and used as prompts for retelling. A collection of suitable artefacts, along with a copy of the book, can be made into a 'story sack', to be taken home and shared with parents.

- **Hot seating**: older children love dressing up as favourite characters and sitting in the 'hot seat' to answer questions from the rest of the group. It's also great fun if adults sometimes dress up and sit in the 'hot seat'. This tends to encourage lots of questioning.

- **Artwork**: well-loved stories can be transformed into pictures, friezes, small-world settings, collages, story books, and so on. Working on these imaginative reconstructions provides many opportunities to return to key vocabulary and to talk about the who, what, where and why of the story.

- **Music, song and dance**: stories or parts of stories can also be turned into action songs, set to music, or turned into mimes and dances (see Chapter 3).

Role-play areas encourage the use of 'story-language'.

Prop boxes for re-enacting stories

Make collections of dressing-up clothes and artefacts to enable children to explore further the ideas and vocabulary introduced during an adult-initiated storytime, for example:

- ✎ *The Three Bears*: a golden wig for Goldilocks; masks for the bears; cones or posts for trees; three bowls and spoons; some porridge oats; three small chairs; and three pieces of carpet for the beds. Make a laminated sign: *The three bears' cottage*. Include the song '*When Goldilocks went to the House of the Bears*' and published versions of the story.
- ✎ *Jack and the Beanstalk*: a very long rope; some pebbles; a packet of seeds; some large boots; and a golden egg. Make some laminated signs saying: *The giant's castle, The beanstalk, Jack's house.*

Make labels to denote characters in the story. Laminate the labels, punch holes in them and thread string through the holes. The children really enjoy wearing the label that matches the character they are playing. Prop boxes are excellent for use outside and stretch the children's imaginations more than a 'static' role-play corner set up inside. The outdoor environment also opens up all kinds of possibilities for acting out stories that would be too messy (or noisy!) inside.

Story treasure hunt

Collect objects that appear in a story you share with the children. For example, if you focus on *Whatever Next?* by Jill Murphy it could be: some Wellington boots, a colander, a teddy bear, an apple, a toy owl, and so on. Hide these objects in the outside area for the children to find.

Small-world play

Set up a 'small-world' scenario that enables children to explore a story further. For example, if you were focusing on *We're Going on a Bear Hunt* by Michael Rosen you might use a series of cat litter trays to represent each stage of the story. (These are extremely cheap to buy and can be used for a wide range of purposes!) In the first tray, sow grass seed in compost to make the long, wavy grass. In the second, put pebbles and shallow water to represent the river. In the third, use clay or compost to represent the mud. In the fourth, stick twigs into lumps of plasticine to represent the forest. In the fifth, use cotton wool and tinfoil to represent the snowstorm. Finally, build a small cave for your bear. A heavy piece of material rolled up with a dim lamp inside can be really effective! Use play people to represent the family and buy an extra copy of the book to cut up and laminate, so the children can sequence the text to match the stages of the story.

Masks and puppets

Build up a collection of masks – some stories lend themselves really well to being re-enacted with masks – for example, *The Gingerbread Boy, Three Billy Goats Gruff* and *Where the Wild Things Are*. And all role play can be carried out on a smaller scale with puppets. Children can make their own, but a suitable collection of hand puppets is ideal for acting out a story like *One Snowy Night* by Nick Butterworth.

Scaffolding children's dramatic play

Perhaps the most powerful thing practitioners can do is to role-play stories *with* the children. At first, children may only take on a small part in the story, but as they watch the adults and gain in confidence they will take on more and more for themselves!

Make your own picture

This is an important listening activity, since it encourages 'mental imaging', which will be important when children come to write stories themselves. Start with a very short, vivid story or poem. Explain that you're not going to show them a picture as you read today – you want them to focus on a blank area (empty whiteboard/blank wall?) and 'make your own pictures in your heads'. When you've read the poem, ask what pictures they imagined. Don't be surprised if at first few respond – children who are constantly fed images on television often do not know how to image in their heads. Talk about the 'pictures in their heads' and ask them to paint or draw their pictures. Repeat the activity, gradually choosing lengthier texts.

Nurturing children's imaginations

Story-telling and listening to stories are key ways of stimulating children's imaginative powers and, as we have illustrated, stories provide a rich context for drama, role play and other creative activities. However, there are many other ways of nurturing children's imagination and stimulating their language, which may also lead into storymaking or the writing of a group poem.

- **What's in the bag?**

  You will need: a feely bag with something interesting inside, for example, some dough inside a plastic bag; some flour secured in a plastic bag; or some sugar cubes or marbles.

  The children sit in a circle and the bag is passed around for them to feel. If it reminds them of anything, if they think they know what it is or if they have a thought to share (or a word to describe what they feel), they speak before they pass the bag on.

- **Play in the field of light**

  You will need: an overhead projector, objects to create a variety of effects, for example, a string bag to create a spider's web, some twigs to create a forest, different coloured slides and overheads to shine into the field of light. Play around with the resources to create different effects. Project the images onto a blank wall or the floor and encourage the children to explore moving in the field of light. Talk with them about all the things it makes them think about and, if appropriate, build on their ideas.

- **Fast and slow music**

  You will need: rolls of paper, such as old wallpaper, markers and a prerecorded tape of contrasting music, for example, slow and gentle, upbeat and loud, choral, classical, jazz, Latin, and so on. Play the music and encourage the children to experience it in any way they like. Some may want to dance and move around the room, whereas others may prefer to use the markers and draw their response. Incorporate the use of fabrics if desired and talk with the children about their thoughts and experiences.

- **Cardboard boxes**

  You will need: a selection of cardboard boxes with holes cut in the sides and top so that the children can 'wear' them.

  The children take turns to 'dress up' in the boxes and use them in any way they like. Share ideas about some of the things they could be used for. The children observing can see if they can guess what is being represented.

- **Duvet movements**

  You will need: an old duvet cover and a PE mat if one is available.

  Spread the duvet cover out on top of the PE mat and get the children to sit around the sides. A few at a time, they can get inside the duvet cover and explore different movements. Encourage the children who are watching to share their ideas about what they were thinking about as they observed the 'movers'.

- **Branches and leaves**

  You will need: branches and leaves that have been discarded when pruning hedges and trees, and some suitable music.

  Play the music and let the children move the branches through space to explore what they will do (having talked through the safety issues with them first!). Generate ideas for other ways in which the branches could be used, for example: to make a den or a shelter, or to role-play a wood or an enchanted forest. Imagine, create and build a story.

Chapter **Five**

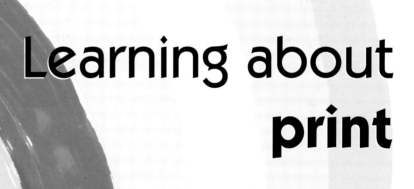

Learning about
print

Learning about print

As long as children have plenty of experience of interactive language, learning to talk is an entirely natural process. In the preceding chapters, we've described many activities designed to build on natural language development – increasing children's spoken vocabulary and ability to express their ideas in words.

However, literacy is **not** natural – reading involves the patterning of complex intellectual behaviour, employing a range of visual, auditory and cognitive skills. Some lucky children learn to read apparently effortlessly through sharing plenty of books with adults – and our 'five a day' routine is designed to exploit this pleasurable way of learning – but we cannot assume this will happen. Many children need a great deal of structured teaching. As for learning to write, which is even more complex – and requires in addition quite taxing physical co-ordination of hand and eye movements – this is hardly ever 'picked up': all children need careful teaching. The remaining chapters of this book cover aspects of written language with which children must be familiar before they can learn to read and write – and the first of these is awareness of the print itself.

To many young children print is invisible – it is so meaningless to them that they don't even notice it. To others it is merely one sort of mysterious squiggle among many – like that of patterns on wallpaper. Children have to learn that print is significant. They have to recognize that *writing* is different from *pictures*, that *words* and *letters* are different from *numbers* – as soon as they start noticing print, those italicized words are important vocabulary to use in context whenever possible.

Children also have to know what reading and writing is for, and how people do it. For instance, in English, print goes from left to right and from the top to the bottom of the page. Finally, they must be familiar with the letters of the alphabet, and how these are used to represent words (see the sections on phonics in Chapter 6). Helping children recognize the nature and functions of print is an important element in laying the foundations of literacy.

Awareness of print

The best introduction to 'the nature and functions of print' is to draw attention to the many examples of **environmental print** that have significance for children in their daily lives. These can be found both inside the setting and out, and are powerful real-life illustrations of the importance of print. The 'listening walks' suggested in Chapter 1 could double as 'print walks', and children's attention be drawn to common notices relevant to them, for example: *Stop, Exit, Fire Exit, Toilets, Playground, Shop, Open, Menu*. Adults should read the words aloud, talk about the sign and why it's there and ensure children know exactly what it means.

The same examples of environmental print (e.g. *Fire Exit*), preferably printed exactly like the conventional sign, should also be displayed wherever relevant in the classroom, preferably at child height. They should also be integrated as often as possible into role-play areas (see opposite for examples). Some signs and notices occur in many contexts, and once children become aware of them, they often take great pleasure in spotting and 'reading' familiar signs for themselves. For many, these become the first 'sight words' – note how the word *out* appears in several common contexts (as a direction, and in the signs for *Checkout, Keep Out, Out of Order*). A child who is familiar with the word in one context can be helped to spot it in lots of others.

Once children have begun to develop phonological awareness, you can also point out initial letter sounds on 'print walks' and in role play, for example: *P* for parking, *L* for learner, *I* for information, *S* and *P* for salt and pepper, *B & B* for Bed and Breakfast, *H* and *C* on hot and cold taps, *M* for McDonald's, and so on.

Ensure key environmental print is at child eye level.

Key environmental print

Shop

No Dogs

Any public building (including early years settings and schools)

Toilets

Outdoor signs

No Parking **STOP** **School** **Litter**

No Entry **Bus Stop** **Playground** **Stop** **Go**

Restaurant /café

No Smoking **Good Food** **Ice Cream**

Alphabet knowledge

An important part of awareness of print is recognizing and being able to name the letters of the alphabet, so it helps to teach children to recite the alphabet as soon as they're able to do so. The easiest way to do this is through an alphabet song, linked to an alphabet chart. Demonstrate the song, pointing to the letters on the chart, and encouraging children to join in until you can hand over the singing to them. Later, you can try stopping as you sing and letting children fill in the missing letter as you point to it. Refer to the letters by their alphabet names (ay, bee, cee) – at this stage, alphabet knowledge has nothing to do with phonics, so this is not a case of /k/ for cat.

Familiarization with the alphabet ensures that children know what *letters* are, and also that there are a limited number of them (without this knowledge, learning to read could seem an impossibly daunting task). If children are interested – especially in the letters of their own names – they may want to play with the shapes, decorating letters, making prints or plasticine letter shapes and so on. Most children are also keen to write their name and, if so, should be helped to do so (see also page 91), but that's as far as *writing* letters should go in the early stages. Long-term success in writing requires adequate fine motor control, hand-eye co-ordination and control of the muscles of the fingers, and starting too early can do more harm than good (see Chapter 7).

The more children play with the letters before learning about reading and writing begins in earnest, the more confident and competent they'll be when they start phonics and, eventually, handwriting.

Making alphabet letters from play dough familiarizes children with their shapes and names.

Dough alphabet

You will need: lots of play dough, some alphabet cutters and a laminated alphabet strip.
As you observe the children playing with the cutters you will be able to learn a great deal about their awareness of print. Some of the children may want to make their names. Encourage those who are ready to match the letters they are making to the alphabet strip. Keep a range of alphabet books nearby so that the children can link their experiences, and sing the alphabet song as you work to encourage yet more links.

Alphabet washing line

You will need: an alphabet frieze, some card, a washing line and some pegs.
Cut up the alphabet frieze, stick the letters onto card and laminate them. You could have upper case letters on one side and lower case letters on the other. This way, children can use the frieze to make their names, sequence letters and make up simple slogans. The added bonus of having laminated cards is that they can be used outside.

Make your own alphabet book

The children are the 'stars' of this book, so they will be motivated to look at it closely. Have the children collect things that begin with A and B and C, and so on. The children who have names beginning with A then have their photograph taken with the collection they have made, and so on through the alphabet. If you have a class mascot or puppet, include him/her in the photographs as this adds even more engagement to the process. This book can then be added to the book corner and the children encouraged to take it home. In fact, try stopping them, when it features them and all their friends.

Alphabet treasure hunt

You will need: wooden or plastic letters and plenty of sand or compost in which to bury the letters.
The children could be set the challenge of finding the letters of their name. If they are not developmentally ready to do this they will just enjoy hunting for the letters and will increase their awareness of the alphabet.

The alphabet thief

You will need: wooden, plastic or magnetic letters.
Lay the letters out in sequence with gaps for where the missing letters should be. Tell the children that someone or something has removed the letters and that an urgent search is required. Prior to doing this you will of course have hidden the missing letters around the setting. This is a great activity for outside as the letters can be tied to the branches of trees and hidden under stones. Hold a celebration when all the letters have been recovered.

Sweetshop alphabet

For this activity, you will need to get the children to collect as many sweet and chocolate wrappers as they can. You will also need a scrapbook.
Talk with the children about which sweets begin with which letter and begin to compile the scrapbook. Don't worry too much if you can't find a wrapper for every letter.

Concepts about literacy

In Chapter 4 we suggested repeated reading aloud ('five a day') of storybooks. With frequent exposure to books in this way, opportunities to look at books themselves in the book corner, and to make their own picture books based on familiar stories and their own experiences, most children will learn all they need to know about 'how books work'. If a few 'five a day' books are available in 'big book' versions, you can occasionally demonstrate some aspects more overtly – for instance, running a finger under the text to illustrate the left-right directionality of print.

However, as well as fiction, children also need you to share and model reading a range of other texts in meaningful contexts – recipes, posters, letters, the phone book, information books, and so on – demonstrating what they're for and how they're organized. Try to take advantage of every opportunity to demonstrate how and why adults read.

Demonstration is also the best way to teach underlying concepts about writing, and shared writing (described on page 94) should happen regularly, with children watching as you write labels and notices for the classroom, parts of letters to parents, captions for pictures, and so on, giving a running commentary on what you are doing.

As they become aware of the significance of print, most children will incorporate reading and writing into their role play – 'pretend reading' menus, phone books, and so on, and 'scribble-writing' notes and messages of various kinds. We can encourage and develop this by ensuring that role-play areas are always suitably equipped with the relevant materials for literacy – health leaflets, posters, magazines, patient notes and 'prescription pads' in the doctor's surgery; brochures, maps, posters and timetables in the travel agents; and so on. For many children, given plenty of encouragement and growing knowledge about the sound-symbol system of English (see Chapters 6 and 7), this emergent reading and writing will develop naturally into 'real' literacy skills.

Role-playing areas can provide many opportunities for 'real-life' reading and writing.

Message boxes and pigeon holes

Buy a supply of 'shoe tidies' and stitch them into one large block that can be suspended from a curtain rail or broom handle. Make sure there are enough spaces for each child and adult to have their own. Stitch laminated photographs of the children onto their space so they can identify their own pigeon hole. They can now use the pigeon holes to exchange tokens, notes and messages.

Abandoned toy

You will need: a soft toy wrapped in a parcel and labelled *Please help me!* and a letter explaining why the toy needs help. Place the parcel somewhere in the outside area for the children to discover. They are usually very excited when they find it. Read the letter inside and let the children dictate a reply. You can then respond to their reply and the correspondence can continue as long as the children remain interested, which is usually quite a long time.

Treasure hunt

You will need: a 'treasure box' containing a small token and a message (e.g. a positive comment) for each child. Find a suitable place to hide it. (If you're really adventurous and have a waterproof box, bury it in the outside area.) Write a letter to the children explaining that there is hidden treasure and a message for them all – it could be from someone they know or a favourite story book character. It should say that to find the treasure they will have to follow a series of clues, and give the location of the first clue. Write and hide the clues. Following the clues until the treasure is found could happen over a day or even a week. Make a display of the clues and the children's individual messages. They usually enjoy reading these to each other.

Television critics

Children are very interested in what has been and is going to be on television. Talk with the children about what's on television that night, and explain that once they've watched it, you're going to ask them what they thought about the programme. Note their responses on a large sheet of paper, which the children can later decorate with pictures cut out from television magazines. In order to fully facilitate this activity, you may need to view the programme yourself – but it is all in a good cause.

Our special character (continued from page 57)

Special characters (soft toys or home-made models) can become the focus of print-based activities. They may receive letters – such as invitations, postcards from friends, official letters requesting them to do something – that spark off another chapter in their adventure. As part of a story, they may need to write letters, lists, signs or notices; you can do this on their behalf. Alternatively, they may need to look up information – for instance in an atlas, reference book, telephone book or recipe book; you can read on their behalf, too. It may be necessary to provide them with documentation – a passport and tickets for a foreign holiday; birth and wedding certificates for happy events; a police statement form in the event of a crime. If they go on holiday, they will probably want to send postcards; on longer trips they may write letters regularly.

Cut-out messages

You will need: a large collection of boxes and wrappers from favourite food. Explain to the children that they are going to cut out words and letters from the wrappers to use as part of a list, poster or notice. Talk about the ways in which the packaging could be used and explore all the various forms of print and text. This is a valuable process in itself and usually generates lots of talk, with the children often noticing subtleties of the packaging of which adults aren't aware. Once you have decided how to use the wrappers, begin cutting and formulate your message.

Sight words

One of the great problems in teaching literacy skills in English is that, due to the vagaries of our spelling system, many commonly used words cannot be decoded or encoded phonetically. Overall, research suggests that the best introduction to reading and writing is through phonics. How, then, does one deal with the fact that words like *the*, *said* and *come* are phonetically irregular? These words must be recognized as wholes, and are commonly called 'sight words'.

We've come to the conclusion that it can be confusing if we draw attention to sight words and phonics at the same time. In terms of explaining how to read and write it is probably best in the early stages to stick to the phonic route, which we outline in the next chapter. However, once children have some grasp of phonics and want to read and write for themselves, no matter how carefully we select reading material, they will soon come up against words that have to be dealt with as wholes.

Children who are frequently read to, and who are used to responding to environmental print, often absorb these commonly used words effortlessly. However, **final** preparation for formal reading should include:

- explaining to children that for some common words phonics doesn't work, and they have to remember how to recognize and spell them as wholes

- games and activities to ensure that all children are familiar with the main sight words (especially those that appear in books they will be reading).

Children who are used to environmental print often learn common sight words easily.

If a word can easily be decoded, children don't need to recognize it as a sight word, so we are surprised that the NLS list of words for Reception classes contains many phonetically regular words. The only words in this list worth teaching as sight words are: *I, look, like, said, you, are, they, come, my, all, was, of, the, to* and two groups: *we, me, she, he* and *no, go*.

To absorb words into the visual memory children need to see them in a variety of contexts, and some children need many more exposures to those words than others. Games are an engaging and fun way of ensuring that exposure and repetition.

Word hunt

You will need: a set of words for each child and a duplicate set that have been hidden in a variety of places.
Children can work individually or collaboratively, and the words can be tailored to their individual or collective needs. Once equipped with their words they set off to find the duplicates. This is a great game for outside!

Card games

These are real old favourites, but the children really do enjoy playing them. Make sight words into bingo, snap and happy families games.

Eat your words!

You will need: some gingerbread dough and some bits and pieces for decorating biscuits.
Give each child in the group a word that you want them to add to their sight vocabulary. Let them make their words from the dough and decorate them. Once they have been cooked they can be displayed and read before they are eaten. Once the biscuits have been eaten, the children can recall who ate which word and find those words in the word bank or on the word wall.

Secret message

You will need: a secret message written in black, which includes some important sight words written in red. (The black words are exposed but the sight words are covered.) The message could give instructions for how to find something that's been lost, to locate hidden treasure or to find out some important information. Explain to the children that in order to 'crack the message', they must carry out certain tasks and each time they complete a task, they can uncover one of the words. You can support the development of a sight vocabulary even further by giving tasks associated with specific words, for example, *'Find the word "they" in five places in the classroom. Find the word "said" in five different books. Find the five "you" cards that are hidden in the classroom.'*
When all the tasks have been carried out and the hidden words uncovered, the children can finally read the message. This activity works well when everyone gets some sort of treat at the end of it. For example, the message might read: *'Go and look behind the cupboard and you will find something that you will like very much!'* or, *'On Friday you can all bring something from home that you would like to show to the rest of the class'*.

Joined-up memory

Sight words must also be learned as wholes for writing. By the time they are introduced, which we believe should be towards the end of the *FoL* programme, most children should be accustomed to writing CVC (consonant – vowel – consonant) words on individual whiteboards (see page 92). Practising writing sight words as wholes – that is, not sounding them out – exploits the kinesthetic learning channel, especially if children are able to write them as joined units. Plenty of practice writing the individual letter shapes (and perhaps joining common digraphs, as recommended by the NLS) should have prepared children to try a few joined words (see the teaching sequence below as an example). The teaching of joins should follow the usual pattern of movement from the shoulder, skywriting and, finally, practice on the whiteboard, all stages of which should be demonstrated, as described in Chapter 7. 'Grown-up' joined-up writing is usually highly motivating for children.

he → the → they

Supporting children's involvement with print

The support provided by the early years practitioner can make the difference between children who simply develop an awareness of print and children who become so fascinated by it that they search for meaning with absorbed intent. Key features of quality support include the following:

- **Observe the children closely**. Watch carefully and notice how children interact with text in all its forms. Notice what they are aware of and what they don't yet understand. Unless we do this, we cannot know what experiences to give them to help them expand their awareness of print.

- **Share your own experience with the children**. Take in the books and magazines that are important to you. Talk with the children about how they give you pleasure and help you in your daily life.

- **Have books and print in all areas of the setting**. Make sure you have text in the construction/sand/water area, and so on, and refer to these texts at every available opportunity. This sends out valuable messages about the importance of print.

- **Enable children to see their own words written down**. Scribe on children's drawings and paintings (with their permission), and let them dictate messages and captions for displays, photographs and home-made books.

- **Encourage children to notice print and use writing in their play**. When you set up any play scenario, mirror the text that would exist in the real world. For example, home corners should always include calendars, magazines and comics, telephone directories, a TV guide, and so on.

- **Include print in the outside area**. Laminate posters of trees, plants and insects to be found in the environment, and screw blackboards to the wall for writing messages.

- **Write down what children plan to do during periods of child-initiated learning**. Talk to children about what they plan and write it on a self-adhesive label so children can wear it. It's a really powerful experience when other adults read the label and say, '*So you're going to play in the sand today!*' At first they ask, '*How do you know that?*' They soon work it out!

- **Encourage book-making activities**. Involve the children in making your own books (like the alphabet book described on page 69). You can make books of children's pictures with your scribed captions, scrapbooks of topics you study, and records of outings and activities illustrated with photographs. Where appropriate, give your books page numbers, front covers, contents pages and back cover 'blurbs' about the content and authors!

- **Let children see YOU writing as often as possible**. Children learn best from the people they love and respect, and because their key adults in their setting are very important to them, they will want to know, understand and copy the things that they do.

- **Talk about what you write with the children**. Whether you are writing a message to another member of staff, filling in a report or recording an observation, tell the children what you are doing and why you are doing it. This will help them to understand that print is something important that helps us to organize our lives. Show them your shopping list and your 'Things to do' list. Get other adults to talk with the children about the things they write and read.

Chapter Six

Tuning into **sound**

Tuning into sound

About twenty years ago, there was a huge change in the way we treat small children. Until then, if a baby or toddler was crotchety, its parent would pick it up, and talk or sing to calm it down. Parent and child made eye contact and shared a cuddle – and in this reassuring context, the child learned the pleasure of listening. What sort of language did parents choose on these occasions? Nursery rhymes and songs, of course – repetitive, patterned language, which just happens to be ideal for tuning a young child's ears to the sounds of speech.

Nowadays, there's another option. After the briefest of cuddles, you prop the child up in front of the television and put on a cartoon. Children love the bright colours and moving images – but the soundtrack is generally lost on them. Nowadays, we tune our children into images, not sounds.

It's just as well our education system brought back the teaching of phonics – without this explicit attention to the sounds that make up words, many children in the last five years might never have learned to read and write at all. However, we still have some way to go in successfully preparing children for phonics teaching. There are a number of developmental stages preceding 'phonemic awareness' (the point at which children realize that you can take a word apart and put it together again: /d/ /o/ /g/ = dog), which children from 'language-poor' backgrounds might not have experienced.

Once phonics teaching begins, children need time to absorb all the data before using it along with all the other cueing systems needed to read a 'real' text. For this reason, we're in accord with synthetic phonics researchers that phonics should be covered in the reception class, 'first and fast', before formal teaching of reading begins. However, we believe children also need plenty of preliminary language play (see page 78) and that when phonics teaching begins at age 5 in reception, it should be 'first, fast **and fun!**' More details on the *Foundations of Literacy* approach to phonics can be found in Appendix 10 (pages 116–19).

Phonological awareness

Phonological awareness means awareness of sounds in language, and is an essential precursor of phonemic awareness – the ability to discriminate individual speech sounds. Children go through a number of developmental stages in phonological awareness:

- **awareness of words** as units of sound. For children from 'language-rich' homes, this happens naturally within the first couple of years, through constant exposure to interactive language. For others, the activities described in Chapters 1–4 should ensure they rapidly reach this stage.

- **awareness of syllables**, that is the recognition that words can consist of more than one sound. Again, for children who engage in plenty of talk, language play and song with adults, this should happen naturally, but the work on 'steady beat' described on pages 42–43 is particularly helpful.

- **awareness of rhyme** (see below).

These 'awarenesses' are completely implicit – children are not aware that they are aware! We can tell that they have reached a certain stage by their linguistic behaviour, especially the degree of pleasure they take in language play.

Rhyme and rhythm

By the time children are able to speak and listen at a level appropriate for the average three year old (see Appendix 1) they are usually aware of rhyme. They enjoy joining in with and learning to recite simple rhymes, and also delight in making up their own (*'It's easy, weasy, peasy, deasy!' 'This is Mr Ooly, Pooly, Dooly, Wooly'*). This is the beginning of phonemic awareness, because the child is gradually alerted to initial sounds (in the examples above, *w, p, d* and *p, d, w*). We should therefore provide, throughout the foundation stage, daily opportunities to join in with, learn and recite rhymes. Appreciation and enjoyment of rhythm underpins awareness of rhyme, and accompanying actions can help make rhymes memorable, so the activities described in Chapter 3 are also very important.

Old MacDonald had a farm...

Children who (despite a language-rich environment and language development appropriate to a 3 year old) do not begin to enjoy and play with *rhyme*, may have a specific learning difficulty (dyslexia). Such problems can now be detected early, so refer any child who concerns you to an educational psychologist.

Down on the farm

You will need: a set of picture cards of different animals.
Shuffle the cards and give one to each child. Explain to the children that once they have looked at their picture, they are to put it face down on their chair or on the floor. On a signal from you, they are to stand up and make the noise of their animal. Explain that the object of the exercise is to find the people who are the same animal as they are. Talk about what they will need to do in order to find their counterparts. You can play this game using zoo animals, vehicles, instruments, and so on. When children start learning phonics, you can adapt it to use with phonemes.

Stories in rhyme

One enjoyable way of developing children's phonological awareness is to include stories written in rhyme in your 'five a day' books. After a few readings they will be joining in, and when they know the text well, you can stop reading at certain key points, allowing them to fill the gaps from memory. You will probably have many such texts in your setting, but some particularly useful ones are:

Bearobics Emily Bolam and Vic Parker (Hodder Children's Books)
Commotion In The Ocean Giles Andreae (Ted Smart)
Five Little Ducks Ian Beck (Orchard)
Giraffes Can't Dance Giles Andreae and Guy Parker-Rees (Ted Smart)
If You Want To Be A Cat Joyce Dunbar and Allan Curless (Macdonald Young Books)
Over In The Meadow Louise Voce (Walker Books)
Pants Nick Sharratt (Orchard)
Pop Goes The Weasel (Macmillan Big Poetry Book)
Row Your Boat Pippa Goodhart (Picture Mammoth)
The Animal Boogie Debbie Harter (Barefoot Paperback)
The Fish Who Could Wish John Bush and Korky Paul (Oxford University Press)
The Lion Who Wanted to Love Giles Andreae and David Wojtowycz (Orchard Books)

Rhymes throughout the day

Make up simple rhymes that can be used throughout the day, for example:

At welcome time:
Hello (insert child's name), how are you today?
It's really nice to see you, is what I'd like to say!

Prior to child-initiated learning:
Who is going to the sand today?
Who is going to the sand?
Who is going to the sand today?
Raise your hand and say!

I am going to the sand today,
I am going to the sand.
I am going to the sand today,
I'm going to the sand to play.

At transition times:
And now it's time to learn some more,
So reach up to the sky, then touch the floor.
Wiggle your fingers and tap your knees
Then clap your hands with a ONE, TWO, THREE!

At tidy up time:
Now we have reached that time of day,
When all the things are put away.
So mind that you all do your share,
Because if you don't it won't be fair!

Find a rhyme and make me squeak

You will need: a toy or puppet with a sound-maker inside (pet shops are a particularly good source).
Sit the children in a circle and encourage them to be inventive and make up words. It doesn't matter if the word is a nonsense word, the skill is to hear the pattern and repeat it. Choose a pattern that has plenty of rhymes, for example: *cat, hat, mat, pat, rat,* or *grumpy, lumpy, bumpy, jumpy,* and so on. Each time someone thinks of a rhyme, the puppet or toy can squeak its appreciation.

See also suggested activities in the NLS *Playing with Sounds* cards, Step 1 (see Recommended resources).

Phonemic awareness

You cannot do enough rhyming activities! However, phonemic awareness will also be developed through alliterative games, tongue twisters and any activities requiring the clear articulation of individual speech sounds. While this can sometimes be done with a large group, discriminative listening really requires small-group attention. All children, therefore, need regular small-group work with an adult – and those whose progress is particularly slow need one-to-one attention.

The general activities outlined above are only a starting point. We have to ensure children can hear and articulate (and eventually remember) the 44 phonemes defined by the National Literacy Strategy (see Appendix 3). The 'Jolly Phonics' technique of associating each sound with an action is a good way to tackle this, as long as it is kept playful and doesn't just turn in to 'phonic drill'. If children are developmentally ready to hear the sounds, they should be able to pick up three or four phonemes and their related actions the first day. You can then return to these daily, playing *'I'll make a sound, you make the action'* and adding further sounds as often as seems appropriate. Once sounds are familiar, you can also play *'I'll make the action, you make the sound'*. It's important to keep careful records of the sounds you have covered, and of individual children's progress. Note that, to begin with, we are talking about **oral** activities (see page 82 for sound-symbol teaching).

The main way that the authors of *Foundations of Literacy* differ from the authors of the *Rose Report* is that we do not believe all children benefit from early **class-based** phonics teaching. Rose also says that teachers should use professional judgement and, for some children, small-group work or individual attention at the appropriate developmental level seems to us more likely to be the correct professional decision.

'Jolly Phonics' actions help children remember phonemes.

What's in the bag?

You will need: a feely bag with some objects inside. (The objects you choose will depend on the phonemes on which you wish to focus.)

Sit the children in a circle and pass the bag around the circle. When you shout 'Stop' or give a similar signal, the child holding the bag draws out an object. They then name the object and pass it onto the next child who tries to think of something else beginning with the same sound. If they cannot think of anything they pass the object to the next child. The object continues around the circle until all the options have been exhausted.

The phoneme walk

You will need: a Dictaphone or a note pad and pencil.

Prior to going for your walk, decide which phoneme you wish to focus on, then set off with the children to spot as many things as you can that begin with that phoneme. When you return, count up how many things you have spotted. Another day, take a walk in a different location and see if you can beat your record. When you can't get outside to do this activity, cut pictures out of old catalogues to play the game.

Wake up the puppet

Explain to the children that your puppet has fallen asleep and can only be woken up when they label an object by its beginning (or final) sound. Show them the object in question and get them to whisper the sound, gradually becoming louder and louder until the puppet wakes up.

Toy box

You will need: a collection of things from around your setting (placed in a box) and several hoops.

Sit the children in a circle and explain that the object of the exercise is to sort out the things in the box according to initial sound and place them in the appropriate hoops. Pass an object around the circle, and on a signal from you, they stop passing. The child with the object selects an item from the box and puts it in the correct hoop, depending on its initial sound. The game continues until all the items have been sorted.

Segment and move

For this activity, explain to the children that you are going to give them a movement instruction saying it bit by bit. Further explain that they are to blend the sounds together to find out what you want them to do. For example, /h/ /o/ /p/, /r/ /u/ /n/, /s/ /k/ /i/ /p/, and so on. Alternatively, sit the children in a circle and put a collection of objects in the middle of the circle. As you segment the sounds, the children take it in turns to identify the object you are referring to.

Change seats

You will need: picture cards beginning with a variety of phonemes.

Sit the children in a circle and shout out instructions, for example '*Everyone who has a picture of something beginning with.... change seats*'. Get the children to continue changing seats until all those children who have pictures of things beginning with the same phoneme are sitting together. You can adapt this game according to the level of phonemic awareness you wish to address, for example:

- ✎ '*all those children who have a word with /a/ in the middle, change seats*'

- ✎ '*all those children who have a word that ends with /n/, change seats*'

See also suggested activities on the NLS Letters and Sounds materials (see Recommended resources).

Phonics: sound–symbol associations

The phonemes of English, as defined by the National Literacy Strategy, and the main ways in which they are represented, are given in Appendix 3. Once children can discriminate, articulate and remember a range of speech sounds (say, the sounds /k/ /a/ /t/ /p/ /i/ /n/ /s/) they should be ready to learn – through games and fun activities – to associate these sounds with specific letters or groups of letters. But always ensure that a phoneme is well established orally before introducing the symbol, and if children do not seem to enjoy the phonic games, go back to oral work until you feel they are secure.

Symbols can be introduced using magnetic letters, lettercards, 'Phonix' cubes (see Recommended resources), and so on. Again, segmenting and blending are an essential element – magnetic letters and 'Phonix' cubes are great for this. The main consideration, however, is that the process should be **fun**. Bored or bewildered children learn only one thing – how to switch off.

Once a sound-symbol relationship is well established, move away from the 'Jolly Phonics' action, and integrate kinesthetic learning through **large-scale** drawing of the letter shapes, starting from the shoulder, then skywriting, and so on (see page 90). Eventually, when children have acquired good hand-eye co-ordination and pencil grip, sounds and words can be written (large) on individual whiteboards (see page 90).

All phonics teaching requires careful planning and record keeping. The children needn't know how structured teaching is, but the practitioner should be working with almost military precision! Obviously there isn't room in this short section to deal with the systematic and thorough teaching of phonic knowledge, but there are now many good commercial schemes on the market, as well as the NLS's *Playing with Sounds* and *Progression in Phonics* materials. Whatever scheme you choose, augment it with fun activities like those opposite, to keep children's interest high. Don't forget the balancing act between the needs of the child and the requirements of the curriculum:

- on the one hand, phonics teaching must be **fun, fast, multisensory** and **cumulative**

- on the other, it has to be addressed **daily, systematically** and **relentlessly**!

About fifteen minutes a day is enough to ensure coverage. However – as the key to this sort of skills learning is 'little and often' – you can also use phonic songs and segmenting games to fill in odd moments, such as transition times, when you're waiting for a website to load, in a queue for dinner, and so on.

The **Letter Fan** game is one of the phonic activities in the NLS Progression in Phonics materials.

Mystery presents

You will need: items that have been wrapped and labelled with their initial phoneme.
Tell the children that you have been given some presents and that you want them to help you guess what they might be from the phoneme on each one. Sit the children in a circle and pass the presents around so they can make their guesses. Record these on the whiteboard (they can help you to sound out the words), then open the presents to see how many they managed to guess correctly.

Missing letters

You will need: a list of words with the initial, medial or final phoneme missing.
Hide the missing phonemes written on cards around the classroom, noting down where each one is hidden. The children look at the first word on the list and try to decide which phoneme is missing. Once they have decided on the most appropriate one, give them some clues as to its whereabouts and they search until it is found.

Place your phoneme

You will need: a collection of artefacts and a bag of phoneme cards.
Get the children to sit in a circle and place the artefacts in the middle. Pass the bag around and when you shout 'Stop', the child holding the bag draws out a card. They then place it next to an artefact that begins with that phoneme. If they have difficulty they seek the assistance of the child sitting next to them.

Highlighter challenge

You will need: some magazines, highlighter pens and a timer.
This is an activity where a small group of children work together to see how many phonemes they can highlight in a given period of time. Give each child some pages from a magazine and tell them which phoneme they are highlighting. At the end of the allotted time, count up how many phonemes they have collectively managed to find. Then give them another phoneme to work on and let them work together to see if they can beat their record.

Post-it play

You will need: a packet of Post-it notes and a 'conch' for passing.
Write some phonemes on Post-it notes and pass the conch around the circle. When you shout 'Stop', the child holding the conch rips off a Post-it note and displays it for everyone to see. The conch is then passed around again, and as each child gets the conch they have to try and think of something beginning with that phoneme. You can also write phonemes that will build into CVC or CCVC words to give practice with blending and segmenting.

Phonics in action – sounds into writing

Alongside games and activities, illustrate how phonic knowledge is put to use during shared writing. For example, 'I want to write "dog". Let's see if we can sound that word out: d/o/g. I know the letters for that' (writing 'dog') or, when reading a regularly spelled word, for instance when pointing out environmental print, 'You know what this says, don't you? STOP. See, it's s/t/o/p.' Do take care, though, not to let phonic encoding take over in any context to the extent that it swamps the meaning.

Phonics in action – Gosh! That's what it's for!

Once children have acquired a reasonable level of phonic knowledge, they usually enjoy decoding some phonetically regular material – it can be quite a thrill suddenly to realise what all these sounds and letters are for! A couple of shared reading sessions, using a big book with phonetically regular text or, even better, the opportunity to decode some little phonic reading books themselves, can often have startling results in terms of children's interest in reading. But don't overdo it, because phonetically regular text is not usually very interesting, and the thrill soon wears off! The key to successful phonics teaching is fun.

See also suggested activities on the NLS Letters and Sounds materials (see Recommended Resources).

Supporting the development of phonic knowledge

Some proponents of synthetic phonics suggest children can learn sound-symbol correspondences without preliminary song and rhyme or other early language activities. We are sceptical about the value of simple decoding skills without a deeper awareness of language patterns and the nature and functions of print. In our experience, for children to read fluently **with comprehension** (rather than merely 'barking at print'), the development of phonemic awareness and phonic knowledge should be embedded in the activities described on pages 78–79 and the other six strands of *FoL*. We should also ensure children have opportunities to build on phonic knowledge during child-initiated learning.

- **Make materials used for focused activities available during periods of child-initiated learning**. Wherever possible, set up an area to include materials that the children can use to play the games they learned at group time.

- **Make up rhymes and jingles as you work with children at play**. This is much easier to do than you may think, and once you get into the habit of doing it you'll find rhymes come to you more and more easily. Such rhymes do not need to be complicated, and children really love it when they are the subject of your rhyme. If you make up simple rhymes consistently the children will pick up the patterns and begin to use them themselves. When jingles relate directly to the children's experience, not only do they take great delight in them, they also find them much easier to remember.

- **Collect rhyming stories and poems**. Rhyming texts are popular with children and great for developing phonemic awareness. The advantage of having a special collection is that you can deliberately select from it on a daily basis.

- **Encourage children to take rhyming texts home**. Ensure there are plenty of rhyming stories and poem books in the 'library box' for home borrowing, including those familiar to the children through your 'five a day' reading. They will love showing off to their parents how well they know the rhymes.

- **Model word building techniques**, not only during shared writing but also as you take down children's words as part of their play. Model also how to decode when you and the children come across an unfamiliar word, such as a sign or poster when you're out on a walk.

- **Provide materials that help to develop phonemic awareness**. Make sure that there are plenty of jigsaws, card games, magnetic letters, letter cutters, 'Phonix' cubes and other resources that children can use during child-initiated learning.

- **Make little phonically regular books available** for children to read, if they wish, during child-initiated activities – and, *if they wish*, to take home to share with parents. Once they are aware of sound-symbol relationships, many children find a real sense of achievement in decoding a little story all by themselves. This must be voluntary, however, as insisting that children decode before they're ready to do so is likely to be counter-productive. Make it clear – for example, by storing the phonically regular books separately – that these are not the same as 'real books'. They are teaching material, the bibliographic version of a jigsaw or card game.

- **Talk with children about the sound and structure of letters and words** and show excitement when they make up rhymes, play with sounds or comment on words and letters. In short, HAVE FUN WITH LANGUAGE!

See also 'Sight words' on page 72.

Chapter Seven

Moving into **writing**

Moving into writing

Writing is the most difficult of the three Rs, as it involves marshalling a wide range of concepts, skills and knowledge. Many activities suggested in previous chapters prepare children for aspects of writing:

- competence and confidence in speaking and listening, a wide vocabulary, well-developed auditory memory and access to a range of expressive language structures (Chapters 1, 2, 3)
- familiarity with the patterns of written language through frequent hearing and repeating of favourite stories (Chapter 4)
- a thorough acquaintance with the alphabet names and letter shapes (Chapter 5)
- understanding of what writing is, what it's for and how phonic knowledge is involved in converting spoken words into printed letters (see Chapters 5 and 6)
- sound phonemic awareness and a firm understanding of the main ways speech sounds are represented in writing (see Chapter 6).

One further aspect needs attention throughout the pre-school years: preparation for the task of manoeuvring a pencil across a page (or a stylus across a tablet PC). In the past, too many children – especially boys – have been asked to perform this fine motor task before they are physically competent to do so. This is demotivating in the extreme and likely to lead to long-term problems with writing, and perhaps literacy in general. We therefore believe strongly that the formal teaching of writing (that is, small-scale, careful writing of letters and words) should be delayed until at least Year 1.

This is not to say that children should not learn about the letters and how to form them. But this learning should start with large-scale movements from the shoulder, which can then be refined into medium-scale movements, such as skywriting in the air using the hand and forearm, and eventually into writing with a marker pen on a small whiteboard, or a chubby pencil on paper. Plenty of practice of letter formation in this way – linked to music, dance and art – provides a secure foundation for the development of neat, fluent handwriting at a later stage.

Handwriting movements

Successful handwriting depends upon secure motor control and hand-eye co-ordination. For some children (especially girls) these skills seem to come fairly naturally; for others (especially boys) they are not natural at all. We have to provide opportunities for all children to succeed in handwriting, by addressing the skills at a variety of physical levels. Throughout the foundation stage, children need plenty of opportunities to develop:

- physical control through large-scale movement, such as outdoor play, balancing, climbing, marching and moving to music

- manipulative skills, such as using tools, cooking utensils and scissors

- fine motor control and hand-eye co-ordination, through activities such as jigsaws, threading, cutting, and manipulating 'small world' equipment.

The three key movements underpinning letter formation – the NLS's curly caterpillar, long ladder and one-armed robot (see *Developing Early Writing* in Further Reading) – should be introduced through large-scale movements, from the shoulder. This can be linked to music and drama, and in the earliest stages children can make the movements symmetrically using both arms (the *Write Dance* programme from the Netherlands, and *Penpals Foundation 1* from Cambridge University Press [see Recommended resources] provide exciting and motivating activities of this kind). Children need considerable practice of each of the three movements at this level, to develop co-ordination and control, and to establish them in kinesthetic memory.

Once a movement is firmly established, you can ask them to try it with the right arm only, again giving plenty of opportunities to practise and 'overlearn' the shape and direction (see Appendix 6 for notes on left-handed children). The next stage is to reduce the scale – for instance, skywriting with the forefinger, or mark-making with sticks in sand, squeezy bottles of water in the playground, wet sponges on a board, and so on. Finally, this shape-making can come down to an even smaller scale, in art activities using felt pens, crayons and chubby pencils.

Write Dance art activities that familiarize children with basic handwriting movements.

Start at the caterpillar's head. Come back and round his back and curl up for his tail.

Come DOWN the long ladder and flick.

DOWN the robot's body. Up and over for his robot arm.

Activities such as the above develop children's confidence and fluency of movement. When possible, encourage them to make shapes using key handwriting movements:

● anti-clockwise curves (the curly caterpillar)
● straight, downward strokes (DOWN the long ladder)
● down, then up and over strokes (the one-armed robot).

Fun with cous cous

You will need: a builder's tray or a sand tray and a plentiful supply of uncooked cous cous.
Pour the cous cous over the bottom of the builder's tray until it is completely covered. Encourage the children to use their fingers to make marks in the grains. Show them how to make a variety of patterns in the cous cous and encourage them to use more than one finger at a time to make multiple tracks through the grains. Make some 'combs' cut from stiff card and add these to the builder's tray. Try this activity with sieved sand, rice or paint that has been applied to the bottom of the tray with a roller. When using grains, pasta and pulses give the children some tweezers with which they can grip and sort the contents of the tray. This will really help to develop fine motor control.

Design your own wallpaper

You will need: some old rolls of wallpaper, decorators' paint brushes, sawn-off broom handles and some paint. THIS ACTIVITY IS BEST DONE OUTSIDE!
Screw the paint brushes to the broom handles and roll out the wallpaper reverse side up. Weight it down with stones if necessary. Show the children how to use the long-handled brushes to make a variety of marks on the paper, and then encourage them to experiment. This activity will really encourage them to 'work from the shoulder'. Try using the brushes to paint on concrete with water and, if you are feeling really adventurous, try painting on the wallpaper with soft nylon-bristled sweeping brushes!

Ever increasing circles

You will need: cat litter trays or similar, sugar paper, salt cellars and plenty of salt.
Line the bottom of the cat trays with black or dark blue sugar paper. Show the children how to fill the salt cellars and use them to make patterns. Start in the middle of the sand tray and pour the salt to make a pattern that spirals out to the edge of the tray. Encourage the children to try the same thing with a square or a rectangle shape. Let them experiment with other shapes, letters and pictures. Once they have poured all the salt from the cellar they can refill it and start again.

While some children (especially girls) have a predisposition towards fine motor skills which fits them for handwriting, they are often less naturally disposed towards gross motor movements and visuo-spatial skills. In our zeal to promote literacy skills, we should not forget to devote time helping these 'natural writers' develop physical and visuo-spatial skills that may not come naturally to them – for instance, the capacity for 'Big Picture thinking', judging distances, spatial awareness and whatever else it is they will one day need to do to park a car satisfactorily.

Letter formation

Children need plenty of time and practice to develop complete control of the three underpinning movements, as described on page 89, before teaching of specific letter formations begins. They should also be thoroughly familiar with the alphabet letters and their names, through activities such as making letter-shapes from pastry, clay or scrunched-up foil (see page 68).

Letter formation can be covered alongside phonics (see page 82). Indeed, practice of the letter-shapes is a useful way of introducing a kinesthetic element into the teaching of sound-symbol relationships, but only if the movement is large-scale. Teaching each letter-shape should therefore start again with large-scale movements from the shoulder. Only when the movement, direction and shape is firmly established should the scale be reduced, through the three stages described on page 88 – but we are not recommending formal handwriting lessons. Throughout the Foundation Stage, the teaching of handwriting skills should be thought of as 'learning through movement', with actual writing of the letters as the ultimate aim.

The letters are best addressed in groups, depending on their formation, and many children benefit from associating each letter formation with a familiar jingle (see Appendix 4). When children are ready to write on small whiteboards, these should be blank on one side, for large-scale practice to develop fluency, but with wide lines on the reverse, as letters' shape, size and orientation depend upon their relationship to the line (the jingles in Appendix 4 refer to the line as 'the ground') – see Recommended Resources for whiteboard supplier.

Letter formation should always be demonstrated with large-scale movements, from the shoulder.

Many children, especially girls, are keen to write at an early age and their mark-making goes through well-established developmental stages (see Appendix 5). Opportunities to write through role play allow them to develop naturally as writers (see pages 70, 71 and 74). Once they are presented with phonic data and shown how this is used to create words, many will progress to 'real writing' just as naturally – often before you cover letter-formation with the group. Such children should not be held back, but they should be given help (individually and as necessary) to ensure they form letters correctly, or they could amass problems for the future.

This page should be read alongside notes in Appendix 6 on left-handed children.

Demonstrating letter formation

Demonstration of letter formation requires at least two practitioners – one to stand at the front (with his/her back to the children) modelling the action. This might be modelling from the shoulder, in the form of skywriting. The children **stand** behind the modeller and mimic the actions. Any other available adults should be behind the children, watching how they go on and gently adjusting their movements as necessary. If it is impossible to provide enough adult help, older children are often very keen to be the demonstrator(s), and it can be a useful way of helping older children with handwriting difficulties to refine their own control of the letter shapes.

Letter formation jingles

Many children find it helpful to hear (and join in with) a consistent jingle to accompany the letter-formation movement (see Appendix 4). The practitioner at the back of the room should take responsibility for saying the jingle, while the demonstrator at the front, like the children, moves in response to it. This means the jingle-speaker can, in the early stages, read the words of the jingle, ensuring they're consistent. As time goes on, the children should become familiar enough with the words to join in.

Writing the letters

Once children are familiar with the letter-shapes and able to make the movements fluently, you can transfer to smaller-scale practice, for instance using:

- paper on easels with stubby crayons or marker pens
- mini-whiteboards and large marker pens.

By this point, it is possible to link letter-formation practice to phonics revision, and we recommend addressing the letters in the groups shown in Appendix 4. Children will continue to need frequent and regular demonstration of letter formation, and a practitioner should always do this with his/her back to the class, so children do not see hand movements in reverse.

Liaising with parents

Stress the importance of careful preparation for handwriting at parents' meetings before children start school, and ask parents not to push handwriting until their children seem keen and interested. However, parents should be aware of the school's handwriting style from as early as possible so they can help at home when appropriate – a handwriting sheet or booklet should be available.

Children usually want to write their names long before the teaching of writing begins in earnest, and often this is taught at home. Provide a card for each parent/carer illustrating the correct letter formation for their child's name, and ask parents to help their child form the letters correctly (and NOT write the whole name in capitals) – otherwise, children might 'overlearn' incorrect movements with every signature. Give out these cards at the earliest opportunity, explaining that there's no rush to teach the signature, but when the child is ready, this is how to do it.

NB: The handwriting style we have used in *Foundations of Literacy* is the Sassoon style recommended by the Primary National Strategy. The letter formation is simple and clear, and leads easily into a joined script as soon as appropriate.

Pencil control

Holding a pencil puts strain on the thumb and first two fingers of the writing hand. If children are asked to write at any length before these muscles are strong enough for comfortable manipulation of the pencil, the act of writing can be physically painful. We believe that many children, especially boys, are put off writing from the very start because of these painful associations.

In any good early years setting there will be numerous resources that will help to strengthen the children's finger muscles as they work with them, but some experiences are better than others (see opposite). There should also be opportunities for children to use crayons, marker pens and chubby pencils, for example:

- drawing, tracing (not handwriting worksheets!), colouring
- emergent writing in role-play situations, using chubby pencils, crayons or marker pens
- eventually, phonics activities, using individual whiteboards and marker pens – children write individual letters and CVC (or later CCVC/CVCC) words in response to the teacher's dictation.

When they are writing, tracing or drawing, help children develop an effective **pencil grip**. The sooner you intervene to stop them from grasping the pencil incorrectly, the less likely they are to 'overlearn' an awkward grip. If they find it difficult to adjust their grip, place the pencil appropriately between their fingers and lightly guide their hand as they draw or trace. Keep the activity light-hearted, praise them immoderately for correct pencil grip, and make light of any regressions – just keep making gentle adjustments.

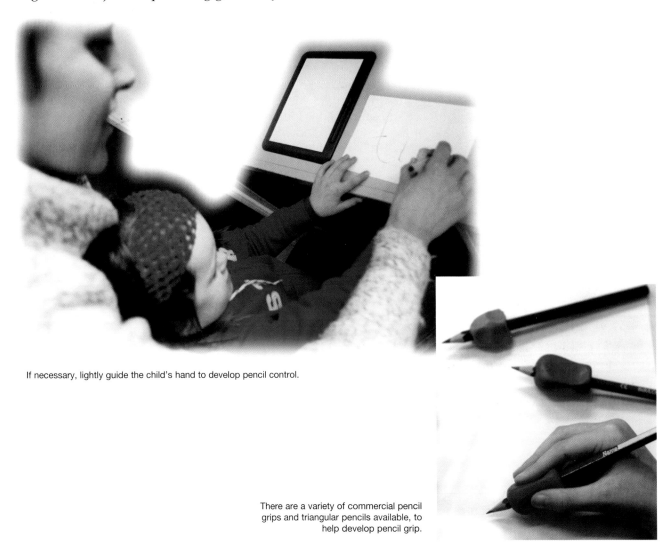

If necessary, lightly guide the child's hand to develop pencil control.

There are a variety of commercial pencil grips and triangular pencils available, to help develop pencil grip.

The finger muscles can be strengthened through many activities – but it's important to ensure there is a range of appropriate materials, so that all children have frequent opportunities to exercise these muscles, no matter what their interests.

Creative activities, for example:

- ✎ painting with fingers and with a wide variety of paint brushes
- ✎ manipulating malleable materials such as dough, plasticine, clay, that can be pounded, rolled, moulded and pinched
- ✎ working creatively with the aid of scissors, staplers, hole punches, treasury tags, recycled materials, and so on
- ✎ sprinkling sand and glitter in the creative area
- ✎ mark-making in a well-equipped mark-making area (see page 96).

Building and making, for example:

- ✎ using woodwork tools, such as screwdrivers, hammers and pliers
- ✎ playing with commercial construction equipment, such as stickle bricks, popoids, brio, mini quadro, interstar, polydrons, and so on
- ✎ weaving, sewing and threading. A bicycle wheel mounted on an outside wall is excellent for large-scale weaving. Alternatively, provide a box of ribbon and fabric and make use of railings!
- ✎ when working with food, using garlic presses, cutters and icing bags.

Sorting and sequencing, for example:

- ✎ picking up and sorting, with fingers or tweezers, collections of pulses, pasta, beads and sequins
- ✎ sorting or sequencing items with pegs on a washing line (e.g. socks, clothes, number, picture or letter cards) – this can be done indoors or out.

Play equipment, for example:

- ✎ collections of nuts and bolts, locks and keys
- ✎ a range of finger puppets
- ✎ a good selection of jigsaws
- ✎ pegboards in a variety of sizes.

Finger rhymes

As well as 'Incy Wincy Spider' there are many rhymes involving finger-play, for example:

> **Here's the church**
> *Here's the church and here's the steeple,*
> *Open the door and here's all the people.*
> *First they sing and then they pray,*
> *And then they quietly walk away.*

Daily routines, for example:

- ✎ helping to prepare fruit and vegetables for snack times
- ✎ putting on and buttoning or zipping coats and other clothes
- ✎ tying bows (e.g. shoelaces, ribbons, ties on aprons).

Ask children who are competent at these skills to help their peers who are still struggling.

Shared writing

In Chapter 5, we recommend regular shared writing as a way of gradually helping children to:

- understand the purposes of writing
- assimilate the relevant vocabulary and the main principles of composition and transcription.

In nursery, shared writing will generally arise informally within child-initiated activities, but a short group session relating to the ongoing life of the setting could happen perhaps once a week. It should be a kind of 'pole-bridged composition' with the emphasis on converting meaning into words or, sometimes, short sentences. By the end of Reception, shared writing with the whole group should be almost a daily activity, involving oral rehearsal of each sentence before writing, and sometimes talk about where to start writing, why we leave spaces between words, and so on. The practitioner should model how to constantly reread what's already been written to maintain the sense. Such sessions should not, however, take more than about fifteen minutes. In Chapter 6 we also suggest that, once phonic work has begun, the practitioner can take the opportunity during shared writing to show how phonic knowledge is used, but never to the extent that emphasis on encoding distracts from the overall meaning.

Shared writing thus becomes a key element in helping children understand the intrinsic nature of composition, and the way all the constituent skills must be orchestrated to put meaning down on paper. At all stages, children should also be encouraged to compose their own sentences and stories, but they do not need to write them down: saying them to a partner or reporting them to the class will be enough. Formal written composition, involving the orchestration of all the skills outlined on page 87, should wait until all the foundations of literacy, including letter formation and pencil control, are in place.

The practitioner can scribe children's contributions to shared writing.

The secret of successful shared writing is to integrate it into the ongoing life of the setting. Use the many 'real' writing opportunities that crop up as a way of demonstrating the significance and importance of the written word – and the many ways it helps us in day-to-day life. Do make sure, however, that you never go on too long. If the shared writing task is a long one, choose which section you will demonstrate, and write the rest at some other time. You might have the start of a letter written up before the shared session, so you can read it to the children and ask them to help you finish it. Or you might write the start of a story and promise to finish it to the children's design. You can then read the whole thing to them later in the day.

Cards and invitations

Most children's earliest encounters with writing are through birthday and Christmas cards, and party invitations. Take opportunities to model how these are written, for example:

- show how to compose an invitation to a party in the setting (e.g. a teddy bears picnic), which you can then have word-processed and duplicated to hand out to each child
- show how to make birthday or Christmas cards to 'our story' characters (see page 57) or to characters in books
- use shared writing to demonstrate how to write *Love + signature* in Mother's Day cards, and so on, when the children are making cards to send home.

Letters, postcards and emails

Use shared writing to compose letters home to give information (you need only model a small part of the letter), or ask children to help you compose a postcard, letter or email to a classmate on long-term absence from school.

Notices and labels for the setting

When you need a new label or sign to be placed around the setting, compose and write it during a shared writing session. Ask pupils to help you find the most appropriate wording. This is a perfect opportunity to demonstrate the importance and consistency of print, as children will then see your writing displayed in context in the setting – and these writing opportunities arise on a regular basis.

Lists, lists, lists

Whenever shopping is required – for parties, for cooking activities, when replenishing any sort of stocks – ask the children to help you compose the list. Similarly, ask children to help you make 'To Do' lists for yourself and for them. Or make lists of children's favourite things: favourite animals, foods, books, television characters, and so on.

Rules and regulations

Use shared writing whenever you and the children need to discuss issues of behaviour. If you involve the children in discussing why things go wrong, how they can be solved, and devising rules to make the life of the setting go more smoothly, they are more likely to remember and abide by those rules. And as they compose them, you can write them out for future display.

Stories and books

When you engage in story-telling activities, as described in Chapter 4, some stories will emerge which become children's favourites. These stories cry out to be written down and illustrated. Do some of the writing as a shared writing activity (not all, as this could get boring), and invite children to provide illustrations to make your own book (either home-made, or using pages stuck in a scrapbook).

Poems

Compose poems on experiences or topics of interest (children suggest ideas, words, lines and you scribe them). As you write them down you can model how to decide when to start a new line, how to keep changing and improving the poem, and other aspects of composition.

Supporting emergent writing

If children are to begin to see themselves as writers, it is essential that we provide them with opportunities to role-play and to make marks and representations on paper.

Encourage mark-making

- provide plenty of opportunities for mark-making outside (playground chalks, blackboards mounted on the wall, painting with water, and so on)
- provide mark-making equipment and large paper in the small-world area so that children can make their own play mats
- encourage children to put as much detail as possible into their drawings (NB drawing is first-draft writing, and children who are still drawing figures where the arms and legs emanate from the head are not ready to begin forming letters!)
- provide a writing area (see below).

Facilitate 'literate' role play

- resource the home corner with materials for children to make shopping lists, write messages, list jobs to be done, write notes for the milkman, and so on
- help children to make pretend registers
- encourage them to make badges, tickets and money as part of their play
- encourage them to write signs and labels as part of their play, such as *The shop is open.*
- in restaurant play areas, help them make menus and price lists and model how to take orders.

Encourage written communication

- encourage them to write instructions, such as *This way to the sand*
- support them to write letters and make cards for parents, friends and family members
- provide message boards, postboxes and pigeonholes, and model how to use them.

Provide reasons for writing

- encourage children to 'sign up' for child-initiated activities
- write notices to which the children can make a response, such as *Who has made some cakes today? Sign here!*
- provide clipboards in the construction and workshop areas so that children can record their ideas

Always have a writing corner

Resources for the writing corner will, to some extent, depend on the amount of space available, but some must be regarded as essential:

- paper in assorted colours, sizes and shapes (paper cut in the shape of vehicles, dinosaurs and space rockets is useful for attracting boys to the area)
- stationery and envelopes
- pens, pencils, felt tip pens, crayons, and so on
- scissors, stapler, hole punch, treasury tags and Sellotape
- message board, postbox, pigeonholes, telephone and note pads
- alphabet chart with examples of upper and lower case letters
- clipboards (Office World sells A5 clipboards that are much easier for young children to handle)
- name card for each of the children.

Where space permits, the following resources are also highly desirable

- labels - calendars - date stamp - Pritt sticks - greetings cards - rulers - rubbers - address books - diaries - pencil sharpeners - typewriter - files - paper clips - bulldog clips - postcards - assorted ready-made books - split pins - calculator - pinboard - elastic bands - and simple dictionaries.

Chapter Eight

Switching on the **searchlights**

Switching on the searchlights

We have described seven strands of teaching and learning which we consider essential before children begin 'formal' literacy learning. By 'formal' learning, we mean:

- shared and guided reading as recommended by the National Literacy Strategy in England
- working through a structured 'reading scheme'
- being expected to *write down* stories, 'news' and other texts
- small-scale practice of handwriting.

In order to succeed in these four activities, children need to orchestrate a wide range of concepts, skills and knowledge, as illustrated in the 'searchlight model' (see below), which underpinned National Literacy Strategy training between 1997 and 2006. Although this model has recently been discredited in terms of early teaching of literacy skills, we believe that (with the addition of a 'physical skills' searchlight) it is still a useful model for describing fluent reading and writing.

However, the early advice of the NLS that teachers should encourage children to 'orchestrate' these four searchlights from the start was – as we have always maintained in *FoL* – inappropriate. For many children, especially those with poor language and listening skills, the cognitive burden was far too great. The seven strands of *FoL* were therefore designed to 'switch on **all** the searchlights' (not just the phonic one!), developing the concepts, skills and knowledge children need *before* they are asked to use them in the complex task of reading and writing.

Attention to each searchlight individually, building up skill in using it through multi-sensory activities – with particular emphasis on oral language – is more likely to lead to confidence and eventual success. Then, when all the searchlights are shining brightly, more formal teaching of literacy skills (e.g. shared and guided reading, handwriting and guided writing) will help children orchestrate them to read and write a variety of texts.

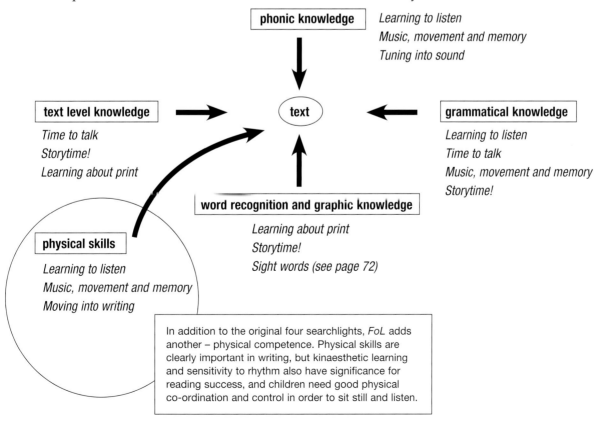

phonic knowledge
Learning to listen
Music, movement and memory
Tuning into sound

text level knowledge
Time to talk
Storytime!
Learning about print

text

grammatical knowledge
Learning to listen
Time to talk
Music, movement and memory
Storytime!

word recognition and graphic knowledge
Learning about print
Storytime!
Sight words (see page 72)

physical skills
Learning to listen
Music, movement and memory
Moving into writing

In addition to the original four searchlights, *FoL* adds another – physical competence. Physical skills are clearly important in writing, but kinaesthetic learning and sensitivity to rhythm also have significance for reading success, and children need good physical co-ordination and control in order to sit still and listen.

The *Foundations of Literacy* curriculum

The *FoL* curriculum is designed for children between the ages of 3 and 6. At each stage, it includes all seven strands of practice, but the emphasis changes as children grow older. In the early stages, practitioners will be concentrating on the development of listening and language skills in general; by the later stages, there is more specific emphasis on the skills underpinning reading and writing.

In the same way, there will be a gradual change in the balance of adult- and child-initiated activities throughout the three years. It is not easy to orchestrate a daily routine where this balance perfectly matches the developmental needs of the children, as the relationship between the two aspects of learning is a dynamic one, requiring great responsiveness from practitioners. Generally speaking, the younger the child, the more *FoL* activities should be woven seamlessly into the fabric of the daily routine. The suggestions on page 103 for integrating *FoL* throughout the day's activities are aimed at 4- to 5-year-old children (in England, the Reception class), but the basic principles hold good for the entire age range. For younger children, timings will probably be slightly shorter; for older children there will be more emphasis on adult-directed activities, although child-initiated activities are still important.

At every stage, *FoL* is consistent with the best pre-school practice. On pages 120–30 (*FoL* guidance section), we show how it overlaps with the developmental milestones and early learning goals and *Practice Guidance for the Early Years Foundation Stage* in England. The practitioners in our trialling schools have found this helpful in planning the work of the setting.

Simple environmental print can be integrated in role play areas from the earliest stages.

FoL curriculum for 3–4 year olds

Listening   daily activities to improve discrimination, develop social listening skills, increase attention span, develop auditory memory (overlap with music and storytime)

Talk   daily spoken language activities, including repeating and innovating on sentences (circle time), targeting selected vocabulary and PREPARE expressive language; activities to compensate for language delay

Music   daily opportunities to keep a steady beat, sing (and learn) songs, action songs and rhymes; frequent opportunities to move rhythmically (e.g. marching, dancing)

Storytime   'Five a day' reading of story books; frequent story-telling sessions; regular opportunities for children to make up stories

Print   frequent attention to environmental print through walks, in classroom, in role-play areas; frequent singing of alphabet song, linked to chart and activities with letters; demonstration of different types of reading

Phonics   Daily rhyme, rhythm and song (link to music); daily rhyming activities

Writing   Activities to develop gross, medium and fine motor skills; large-scale handwriting movement activities (link to music, drama, art); attention to pencil grip; occasional relevant shared writing

FoL curriculum for 4–5 year olds

Listening   daily activities to improve discrimination, develop social listening skills, increase attention span, develop auditory memory (overlap with music and storytime, phonics); weekly learning of a simple rhyme

Talk   daily spoken language activities, including repeating and innovating on sentences (circle time), targeting selected vocabulary and PREPARE expressive language; activities to compensate for language delay

Music   regular opportunities to develop rhythm, sing (and learn) songs, action songs and rhymes; frequent opportunities to move rhythmically (e.g. marching, dancing)

Storytime   'Five a day' reading of story books; frequent story-telling sessions; regular opportunities for children to make up stories

Print   frequent attention to environmental print; gradual linking of alphabet knowledge to phonics; demonstration of different types of reading

Phonics   Daily rhyme, rhythm and song (link to music); daily oral activities to learn phonemes and use them to segment and blend; later, daily phonic activities, using magnetic letters or other concrete materials; integration of phonic knowledge into shared writing

Writing   Large-scale letter formation (link to music, drama, art); frequent large-scale practice of letter formation; attention to pencil grip and handedness; daily shared writing

FoL curriculum for 5–6 year olds

Listening   daily activities to develop attention span and auditory memory (overlap with music and storytime, phonics); weekly learning of a simple rhyme

Talk   daily spoken language activities, including repeating and innovating on sentences (circle time and storytime), targeting of selected vocabulary and PREPARE expressive language; activities to compensate for language delay

Music   regular opportunities to develop rhythm, sing (and learn) songs, action songs and rhymes; frequent opportunities to move rhythmically (e.g. marching, dancing)

Storytime   'Five a day' reading of story books and frequent story-telling sessions, with emphasis on children's retelling of stories; regular opportunities for children to make up stories

Print   frequent attention to environmental print; linking of alphabet knowledge to phonics; demonstration of different types of reading; sight word activities

Phonics   Daily rhyme, rhythm and song (link to music); daily phonic activities, using magnetic letters or other concrete materials and linking to letter formation; reading, when children are ready, of phonically regular material; integration of phonic knowledge into shared writing

Writing   Frequent practice of letter formation; attention to pencil grip and handedness; daily shared writing

Fitting it in

The guidance for the Early Years Foundation Stage in England clearly states that the best possible daily routine for 3, 4 and 5 year olds involves an appropriate balance between adult- and child-initiated activities. For young children, learning cannot be compartmentalized, so practitioners need to be highly skilled at ensuring that the foundations for literacy are built into every aspect of the daily routine.

In order to do this effectively, we suggest practitioners plan for children's learning on a term-by-term, week-by-week, day-by-day and hour-by-hour basis, paying close attention to how the seven strands of the curriculum are woven throughout the day's activities and across the areas of learning. As many opportunities arise in response to the children's current interests and motivations, and are therefore difficult to plan for, practitioners should carry out regular audits (see audit sheets, Appendices 7–9).

All settings are different and necessarily manage time, space, people and the daily routine in ways that best suit their individual needs. However, there are elements that are common to all settings, and the list of elements of a Reception day given on the opposite page gives examples of how the *FoL* curriculum can be woven throughout these elements. Although this list was originally devised for 4 to 5 year olds, the elements do not differ greatly from those found in a nursery setting or the first term of a Year 1 class. In the nursery setting, adult-directed activities will probably be shorter and simpler, while throughout the course of Reception and Year 1 they will become increasingly complex and extended, as the children become more able to concentrate on an adult agenda.

Creative role play provides opportunity for vocabulary and expressive language development at all ages.

Welcome time (10–15 minutes)

This provides opportunities for many types of *FoL* behaviour, for example: adults model respectful listening as they greet children and parents; practitioners, children and parents converse and chat; children use their name cards to self-register; adults and children use the message board to note down things that are important to remember and relevant to the day; children sing a song, make up a rap or finger rhyme as others arrive; children select books and activities with which to work until welcome time is over.

Focused activity time (10–20 minutes)

The length of focused activity time varies, depending on children's developmental level. When it has a *Communication, Language and Literacy* focus, it could involve listening games; circle time activities; role-play activities; phonic games; print-based activities; steady beat sessions; shared writing; gross motor activities outside; focused time in the mark-making area; handwriting activities involving music, movement, drama and art. When the focus revolves around another area of the learning, there may still be opportunities for literacy development (see pages 120–30).

Snack time (10–15 minutes)

This part of the daily routine provides many opportunities for social language and listening.

Planning for periods of child-initiated learning (5–10 minutes)

When children are thinking about and planning for how they will spend their time, there are opportunities for them to share their plans in pairs; see their ideas being written down by an adult; make up raps about who is going to do what; speak their plans into a Dictaphone or tape recorder; draw and talk about their plans.

Child-initiated learning (at least 45 minutes)

As children work at their own self-directed activities, you can listen, talk, use rhyme, make music, role-play with and write for them. All this should be done in a way that complements and does not interrupt their play. It helps to make posters of the key elements of the *FoL* curriculum (see Appendix 2) and put them around the setting as an aide-memoire. After a while, the process will become so second nature that you won't need to refer to the posters at all.

Tidy-up time (5–10 minutes)

Tidy-up time offers opportunities for singing, rhyming, rapping and musical activities. You can play music with a strong beat as a background to the whole process, or play marching music and march from one place to another as you put things away.

Review time/plenary (10 minutes)

The opportunities at planning time are again available during review of child-initiated learning.

Whole-class activities (approx 15 minutes)

The opportunity for children to meet in a large group might involve: stories (several short books can be read within one session); circle time activities (talk and listening); action rhymes and songs; listening games; shared writing activities, steady beat, rhythm, music and movement activities.

Transition times

As each part of the daily routine comes to an end and gives way to a new activity, you can use a rap, rhyme or song that relates to what you have just done or something you are about to become involved in. Marching or skipping from one place to another helps develop basic timing!

Story and home time (10–15 minutes)

Preparing for the end of the day is a further opportunity to gather for stories and song. If there are letters to be given out, talk about their purpose with the children and, where appropriate, encourage them to ask questions about their content.

Creating the culture

On page 99 and in the audit sheets in Appendices 7–9, we outline the elements of the *FoL* curriculum relevant for children at different stages between the ages of 3 and 6. However, the experience children bring to a setting varies greatly, so there may be a wide range of ability. Some children will find *FoL* activities relatively easy; others may find them challenging and need plenty of one-to-one help and encouragement. Some groups may, on the whole, be able to move rapidly through the programme; others will need gradual, incremental encouragement, with plenty of consolidation at each stage. Practitioners must use their own experience and expertise to assess the speed with which to proceed.

We believe the key element in creating the *FoL* culture is to value the skills of speaking and listening. For far too long these have been taken for granted in British settings and schools, and their huge importance in all learning has simply not been recognized. We believe this is the main reason for our difficulties in raising literacy standards, especially among those children who do not come from 'language-rich' backgrounds. Our educational ethos requires us to press on with literacy skills at the earliest possible opportunity, and the whole of our national culture reflects this ethos. It's therefore extremely important that we explain *FoL* clearly to parents, so they do not fear we are 'holding their children back'.

Elsewhere in Europe, as in America, it's considered extremely important that children speak up and speak out. Spoken language activities are a valued part of education throughout their school careers. What's more, the two countries which, in international studies, have the greatest success in literacy – Sweden and Finland – have a completely oral curriculum until children are 7 years old. Here in the UK, we must get away from the idea that sitting silently 'on the mat' while the teacher tortures a big book, or ploughing through a reading scheme at an early age, or struggling to write a story when they can hardly hold a pencil, are somehow 'good for children'.

The seven strands of *FoL* – with their constant emphasis on speaking and listening – not only provide the building blocks for literacy so that, once formal teaching begins, more children succeed and fewer fail. They also focus on the enjoyment and appreciation of literacy, so that children **want** to read and write, and will thus develop their literacy skills through willing practice. Perhaps most important of all, they provide the basis of an essential life-skill which we ignore at our peril – the ability to explore and express our ideas through language, and to communicate our needs and feelings to others. It is the development of these skills, in all our citizens, upon which society ultimately depends.

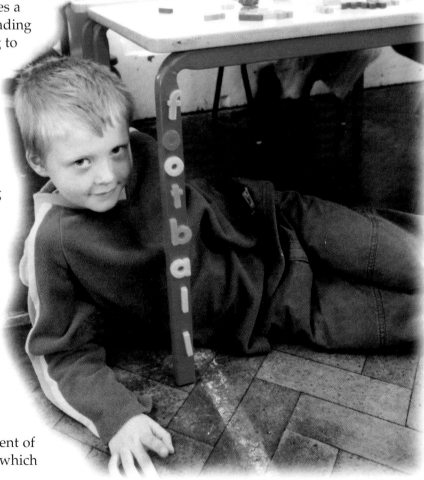

Self-confident motivated children learn to write because they want to.

Little by little

When introducing *FoL*, don't try to do everything at once. Focus on each strand of the *FoL* curriculum in turn and consider how it can be developed in your setting through each aspect of the daily routine (see page 101). Focus on a strand for one week, becoming aware of what works well and what doesn't. Once you have been through this process, you will be in a position to **do more of what works on purpose**! Then move on to consider another strand of *FoL* in the same systematic way until you have covered all of them. When you have done this, use the appropriate audit sheet (see Appendices 7–9) on a weekly basis to check out that all strands of the curriculum are receiving sufficient attention. Once you are clear that everything is receiving systematic attention you will need to audit less often. However, the *FoL* curriculum in this book is merely a starting point. Until the website is established, you can contact us via FoL@suepalmer.co.uk and please, if you come up with something that works, let us know!

Little and often

Children in the nursery phase of early education need very short sessions of adult-initiated activities, increasing in length as their concentration spans develop. These short sessions should be spread throughout the day (see page 101). As they grow older, children should be able to maintain attention during adult-initiated activities for longer, but practitioners should always be alert to the group's attention. If you feel you've lost them, there's no point in continuing with an activity. Try something else (a song or action rhyme or perhaps a session of Brain Gym®) and see if it revives concentration. If not, don't go on flogging the dead horse a moment longer – whatever you're doing clearly doesn't work and you need to rethink!

Sitting and moving

Small children cannot sit still for long, and many adult-initiated activities involve a certain amount of sitting 'on the mat'. As suggested above, it's important that relatively passive activities are interwoven with more active ones. For instance, during an adult-directed session, once you've finished a circle time sentence-completion activity, ask children to stand up for some music and movement. However, research suggests that, during circle time and other talk-based, whole-group work, children find it easier to concentrate if they are sitting on small chairs, rather than 'on the mat'. Is there any way, within your setting, of providing both comfortable seating **and** room to move during adult-initiated sessions?

On location

Go 'on location' as often as possible, by conducting adult-initiated sessions in the role-play area, water area, sand area, creative area, outside area, and so on. This enables you to model the types of play and language that are possible and appropriate, and once children are aware of the possibilities, they will return during periods of child-initiated learning and build on what you have modelled. Pay careful attention to how your team is developing children's language during play (see Chapter 2: Time to talk).

It's good to talk

Teach conflict resolution. When young children are in conflict over space, materials or friends, teach them how to:

- acknowledge their feelings in a difficult situation
- gather information by restating what has happened
- generate possible solutions and choose one together (and once they have done this, make sure you offer any necessary follow-up support).

As well as developing language and social skills, this helps children see – in the most meaningful of contexts – that speaking and listening are extraordinarily useful on a day-to-day basis. It's not overstating the case to say that the ability to resolve conflicts in this way underlies the institutions of our democratic system.

Smooth transitions

It is difficult to specify exactly when 'formal' literacy should begin. For some groups of children – for instance, children from language-rich backgrounds where many of the activities we describe are familiar before they enter school – the majority may well be secure in all seven strands by the end of the Reception year. For others, it may be that another full year should be devoted to the *Foundations of Literacy* curriculum, and formal literacy should not begin until some time in Year 2. Our feeling is that most children would benefit from following the sort of course we have described until they are at least 6 years old. In England, that would probably be the beginning of Year 1 Term 2.

Some children in any group will, of course, start reading and writing before they are 6 through their own emergent literacy activities. They should be encouraged, their efforts celebrated and individual help provided (for instance you should ensure letters are correctly formed, by linking to what you're doing in the *Moving into writing* strand). These children can then form a 'top group' once formal learning starts. But in the meantime they too will benefit from a whole-class emphasis on speaking, listening, music and social skills, along with a more informal approach to their interest in reading and writing.

Whenever the transition occurs, it needs to be treated as a whole-school issue so that senior managers and the rest of the staff understand and give their support to the process. There should also be careful consideration to sharing this process with parents, who must also understand why you are doing things in the way you have agreed.

Initially, when children move from the foundation to the national curriculum, both the physical environment and the daily routine should mirror, to the greatest possible extent, what children have experienced during the foundation stage. Key Stage 1 children still need access to a quality play curriculum and will develop literacy skills far more effectively when this is present. But they need more challenging resources, more complex problems to tussle with, and they need to develop more sophisticated language with which to explore their ideas.

This is why we recommend making the transition during the course of Year 1, so that a familiar teacher helps them move from one type of practice to another, with the minimum of 'culture shock'. The secret of success lies in beginning with what they know and are confident with, and then, through a gradual process, building on those opportunities to increase the level of challenge and complexity. As Year 1 progresses, teachers should ask themselves:

- do we currently make the best possible use of the role-play area, construction materials, 'small world' resources, and so on?
- have we extended the periods of adult-initiated learning as the year progresses?
- do we nevertheless still support children working on their own self-initiated activities?
- do we promote independent learning so that children become skilled at using a task board and taking responsibility for their own learning?
- do we involve the children in decisions about how the classroom is organized and share responsibility for its smooth running?
- do we integrate movement/Brain Gym® work into the daily routine (especially important when working in a small classroom with restricted space)?
- are there any ways of recruiting more adult help into the classroom, for example by training some NVQ students, appealing to parents, friends and grandparents?
- are all areas of the *FoL* curriculum still receiving appropriate attention (see audit sheet in Appendix 9)?

Appendix 1: Language development

Normal development of expressive language

Approximate age	Type of talk	Examples
0–1 (the first year)	- babble - early attempts at words	*Dada*
1–2 (the second year)	- more recognizable words - lots of repeated words - sometimes puts two words together - uses question intonation - by 18 months, knows up to 50 words, by 2 years old up to 200 - 2/3 words together in short sentences - starts using question words	*Bye-bye* *Oggy-oggy* *Daddy there?* words for actions, food, body parts, clothes, animals, vehicles, places, pronouns, colour, shape *That my house* *What that noise?*
2–3 (the third year)	- puts together sentences of 3, 4 and more words - uses word endings, e.g. plurals, tense - possibly 500 words by two and a half years old; 1,000 by 3 years old - period of intense questioning - use of *and* to link ideas	Me got cars. *Daddy comed see me in garden.* *Why? Why? Why?* *I want juice and bikky!*
3–4 (the fourth year)	- produces increasingly long sentences - little words like *to* and *the* appear - links ideas using, e.g. *when, cos, after, before* - uses language for a variety of reasons, including: retelling favourite stories, role play and 'pretend', recounting events - vocabulary of up to 5,000 words	*We wented to town and we did have a haircut and then we got a Big Mac.* *I go now cos my mummy's here.* *I eated it when I watched the telly.* *You be the baby and I'll be the mummy. You sit here and I'll go and get your juice. Be good or you won't get no juice.*

Normal development of articulation

Approximate age	Consonant sounds	Speech
9 months–2 years	m, n p, b, t, d w (k, g)	- repeated syllables e.g. *Dada* - final sounds missed off words e.g. *do* for *dog* - recognizable words e.g. *tat* for *cat* - *k* and *g* not used all the time
2 years–3 years	ng, k, g (f, s) h	- final sounds still sometimes omitted e.g. *Go to tea-tie* (sea-side) - *f* and *s* sometimes used
3 years–4 years	f, s v, z sh, ch, j l	- words usually have final sound, but not always the adult one, e.g. *fiss* for *fish* - *sh, ch, j* develop later - where there are two consonants together, the child may use only one, e.g. *no* for *snow*
4 years onwards	th, r, zh	
7 years onwards	Mature pronunciation of most words	

Appendix 2: PREPARE chart

TIME TO TALK: PREPARE

Plan
Let's think about what we/you are going to do.
I wonder what we'll need? Tell me how you'll start.
What do you think you'll do next

Thinking ahead
Sorting out sequence
First, Next, Then.., etc.

Recount
Can you remember what happened when...?
Where were you? Tell me how it all started.
What happened next? How did it all end?

Thinking back
Working out sequence
In the beginning...

Explore
I wonder what this is? What might that be for?
I wonder how it works? I can't guess what this does – do you have any ideas? Where do you think this should go?

Considering possibility
in the here and now
Tentativeness: *I think...; Maybe*

Predict
I wonder what's going to happen?
Can you guess what will happen next?
What do you think would happen if...? (or if we didn't...)

Anticipating the future
based on what you
know. Tentativeness

Analyse
Gosh – what's going on here? Can you work out how this happened? Do you notice anything about...?
Why do you think it happened? How did you feel when...?

Consciousness of
observation. Curiosity.
Reflection on feelings

Report
Tell me about... What is it for? What does it do?
What colour/shape/size is it?
What does it look/sound/feel/taste/smell like?

Observation and
explicitness; awareness
of key features

Explain
Do you know how this works? I wonder why that happens?
What starts it off? Do you know what makes it do that?
Do you know the reason for...? How do we know that?

Curiosity: how and why?
Awareness of sequence
Cause and effect

Appendix 3: The phonemes of English

(as defined by the National Literacy Strategy in *Progression in Phonics*)

Consonant phonemes with consistent spellings

/b/   **b**at, ra**bb**it

/d/   **d**og, da**dd**y

/g/   **g**irl, gi**gg**le

/h/   **h**ot

/l/   **l**og, lo**ll**y

/m/   **m**at, su**mm**er

/n/   **n**ut, di**nn**er

/p/   **p**ig, su**pp**er

/r/   **r**at, ca**rr**y

/t/   **t**op, pa**tt**er

/y/   **y**ellow

/th/ **th**is (voiced) **th**ing (unvoiced)

Consonant phonemes with alternative spellings

/k/   **c**at, **k**ing, ba**ck**, s**ch**ool, **q**ueen

      (also the /k/ sound in bo**x**)

/s/   **s**un, pre**ss**, **c**ircle

/f/   **f**un, **ph**oto

/j/   **j**am, **g**inger, bri**dge**

/w/   **w**orm, q**u**een

/z/   **z**oo, pin**s**, **x**ylophone

/v/   **v**an (one exception: o**f**)

/sh/ **sh**eep, sta**ti**on, **ch**ef

/ch/ **ch**in, i**tch**

/ng/ si**ng**, pi**n**k

/zh/ mea**s**ure, a**z**ure

'Short' and 'long' vowel phonemes

/a/   b**a**g

/e/   b**e**t, br**ea**d, s**ai**d

/i/   b**i**g, c**y**linder

/o/   t**o**p, w**a**s

/u/   b**u**n, l**o**ve

/ae/ d**ay**, p**ai**n, g**a**te, gr**ea**t

/ee/ f**ee**t, s**ea**t, P**e**te, m**e**

/ie/ t**ie**, t**igh**t, fl**y**, t**i**me

/oa/ b**oa**t, gr**ow**, b**o**ne, t**oe**, g**o**

/ue/ bl**ue**, m**oo**n, gr**ew**, fl**u**te, y**ou**

Other vowel phonemes

/oo/ g**oo**d, p**u**t, c**ou**ld, w**o**lf

/ur/ ch**ur**ch, b**ir**d, h**er**b, **ear**th, w**or**d

/ar/ st**ar**t, f**a**ther

/or/ c**or**n, d**oor**, sh**ore**, r**oar**, y**our**,

      p**aw**, t**au**t, t**a**ll, t**a**lk, t**augh**t

/ow/ cl**ow**n, sh**ou**t

/oy/ b**oy**, **oi**l

/ear/ n**ear**, d**eer**, h**ere**

/air/ ch**air**, sh**are**, th**ere**

/ure/ p**ure**, t**our**ist

'schwa' (an indeterminate 'uh'

sound) farm**er**, doct**or**, gramm**ar**,

met**re**, col**our**, Americ**a**.....

NLS suggests teachers ensure children can first hear a phoneme, then introduce one way of writing it (i.e. the first spelling pattern given in each list of examples). Other main spelling patterns can be introduced, as required, widening the spelling choices.

Appendix 4: Handwriting groups and jingles for large-scale practice

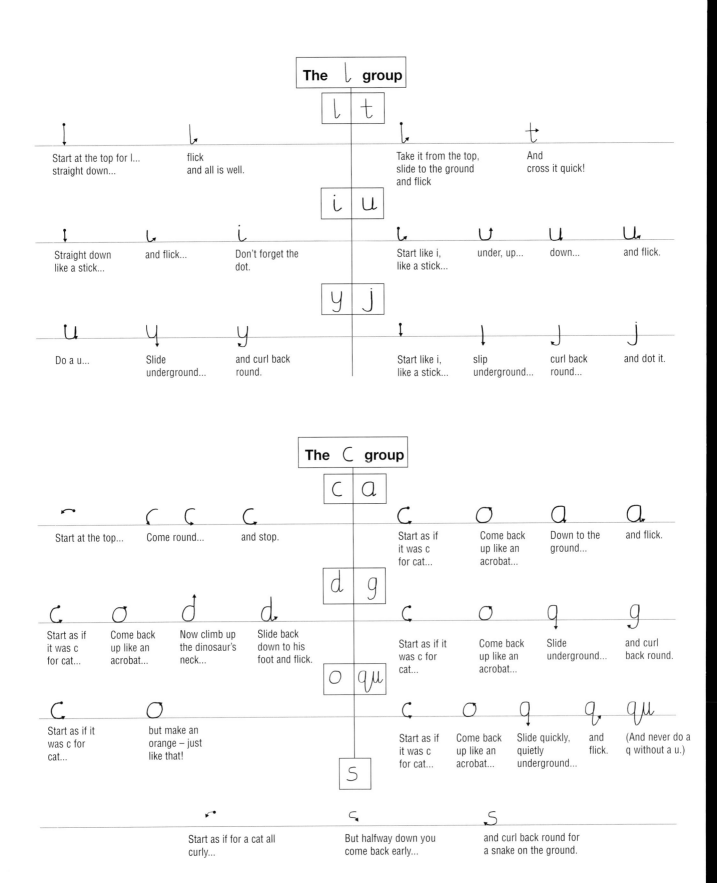

The *l* group

| *l* | *t* |

Start at the top for l... straight down...   flick and all is well.   Take it from the top, slide to the ground and flick   And cross it quick!

| *i* | *u* |

Straight down like a stick...   and flick...   Don't forget the dot.   Start like i, like a stick...   under, up...   down...   and flick.

| *y* | *j* |

Do a u...   Slide underground...   and curl back round.   Start like i, like a stick...   slip underground...   curl back round...   and dot it.

The *c* group

| *c* | *a* |

Start at the top...   Come round...   and stop.   Start as if it was c for cat...   Come back up like an acrobat...   Down to the ground...   and flick.

| *d* | *g* |

Start as if it was c for cat...   Come back up like an acrobat...   Now climb up the dinosaur's neck...   Slide back down to his foot and flick.   Start as if it was c for cat...   Come back up like an acrobat...   Slide underground...   and curl back round.

| *o* | *qu* |

Start as if it was c for cat...   but make an orange – just like that!   Start as if it was c for cat...   Come back up like an acrobat...   Slide quickly, quietly underground...   and flick.   (And never do a q without a u.)

| *s* |

Start as if for a cat all curly...   But halfway down you come back early...   and curl back round for a snake on the ground.

Foundations of Literacy © Sue Palmer and Ros Bayley

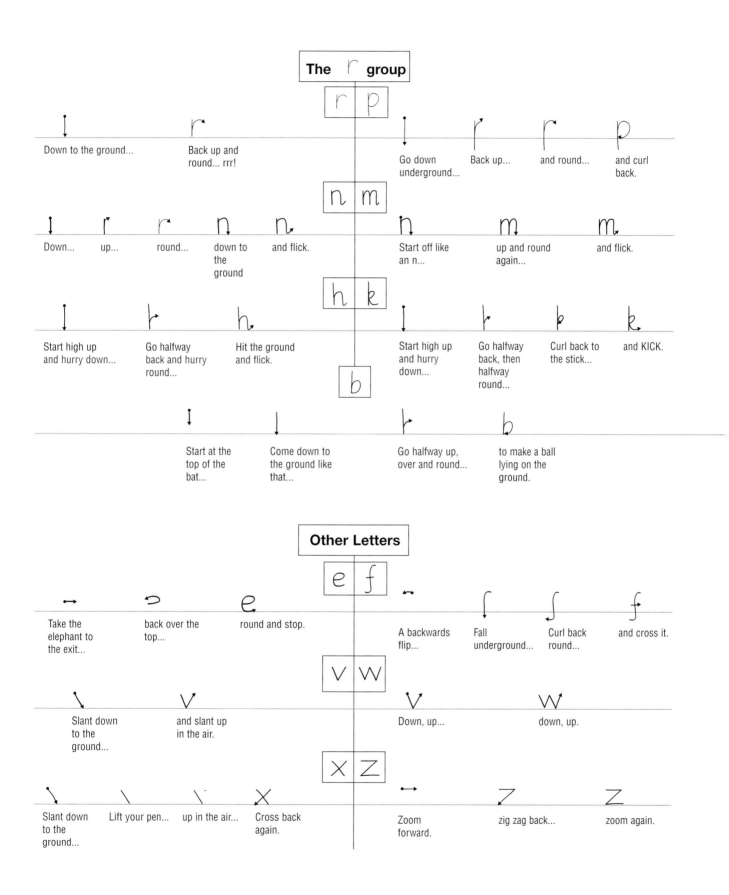

The r group

r p

Down to the ground... | Back up and round... rrr!

Go down underground... | Back up... | and round... | and curl back.

n m

Down... | up... | round... | down to the ground | and flick.

Start off like an n... | up and round again... | and flick.

h k

Start high up and hurry down... | Go halfway back and hurry round... | Hit the ground and flick.

Start high up and hurry down... | Go halfway back, then halfway round... | Curl back to the stick... | and KICK.

b

Start at the top of the bat... | Come down to the ground like that...

Go halfway up, over and round... | to make a ball lying on the ground.

Other Letters

e f

Take the elephant to the exit... | back over the top... | round and stop.

A backwards flip... | Fall underground... | Curl back round... | and cross it.

v w

Slant down to the ground... | and slant up in the air.

Down, up... | down, up.

x z

Slant down to the ground... | Lift your pen... | up in the air... | Cross back again.

Zoom forward. | zig zag back... | zoom again.

Appendix 5: Stages in emergent writing

This developmental checklist, taken from the NLS training materials for teaching assistants, provides a guide to the normal developmental progression of handwriting and phonic skills in children's emergent writing. Progress will be accelerated if practitioners provide pointers and models (through the type of commentary chosen during shared writing and individual help during child-initiated learning) of the next stage. As children learn phonics and letter formation, we should expect to see this feed into their emergent writing.

- Random scribble
- Scribble that looks like writing
- Individual shapes that look like letters
- Some real letters used randomly (especially letters from own name)
- Letters and shapes written from left to right across the page
- Individual letters used to represent words (usually initial sounds)
- More than one letter used to represent a word (usually significant consonant sounds; in CVC words the first and last letters)

Appendix 6: Left-handed children

Approximately 12 per cent of the population are left-handed, so there's a good chance of having a few left-handers in every class of 30 children. Boys are more likely to be left-handed than girls. If a child is left-handed, any attempt to force him or her to use the right hand could cause long-term psychological damage. However, many children take quite a while working out which is their preferred hand, and some are genuinely ambidextrous. If a child seems happy to work with either hand, try gently to guide them towards the right – it's definitely easier to be right-handed in a right-handed world.

Watch children carefully to gauge any genuine left-handers. Ensure you have some left-handed scissors so that they aren't handicapped when learning to cut out. When the time comes for help with basic handwriting movements, letter formation and, eventually, handwriting itself, they need special attention. If at all possible, don't ask them to join in with the right-handers' lessons. It's better if they can go off and have a special lesson of their own – if there's a left-handed adult to model for them, that's ideal, but otherwise someone will have to train themselves to teach the movements left-handed. Later, when children are taught to write, the teacher should again model left-handed writing, and give opportunities to talk about any difficulties.

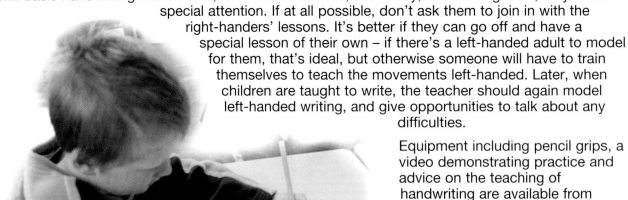

Equipment including pencil grips, a video demonstrating practice and advice on the teaching of handwriting are available from Anything Left-handed (see Chapter 7: Recommended resources). Try to ensure that left-handers are seated so there is space on their left-hand side – otherwise they tend to collide with right-handers coming from the opposite direction!

Pencil grip and paper slant for left-handed writers.

Appendix 7: *FoL* audit sheet for practitioners working with 3–4 year olds

Listening

daily activities to improve discrimination ☐

daily activities to develop social listening skills ☐

daily activities to increase attention span (overlap with music and storytime) ☐

daily activities to develop auditory memory (overlap with music and storytime) ☐

Talk

daily spoken language activities, including repeating and innovating on sentences ☐

daily targeting of selected vocabulary (changed weekly) ☐

targeting of PREPARE expressive language in adult- and child-initiated activities ☐

daily conversations compensating for language delay ☐

daily talk during child-initiated activities ☐

Music

daily opportunities to keep a steady beat ☐

daily opportunities to sing (and learn) songs, action songs and rhymes ☐

frequent opportunities to move rhythmically (e.g. marching, skipping, dancing) ☐

Storytime

'five a day' reading of story books ☐

frequent story-telling sessions ☐

regular opportunities for children to make up stories ☐

Print

occasional environmental print walks ☐

environmental print displayed (and discussed) in classroom ☐

appropriate environmental print in role-play areas ☐

frequent singing of alphabet song, linked to chart ☐

regular activities with letters (including writing name) ☐

occasional demonstration of different types of reading ☐

Phonics

daily rhyme, rhythm and song (link to music) ☐

daily rhyming activities ☐

if appropriate, introduction of phonemic awareness activities ☐

Writing

daily activities available to develop gross, medium and fine motor skills ☐

large-scale handwriting movement activities (link to music, drama, art) ☐

attention to pencil grip when children use pencils ☐

occasional relevant shared writing ☐

Appendix 8: *FoL* audit sheet for practitioners working with 4–5 year olds

Listening

daily activities to improve discrimination ☐

daily activities to develop social listening skills ☐

daily activities to increase attention span (overlap with music, storytime, phonics) ☐

daily activities to develop auditory memory (overlap with music, storytime, phonics) ☐

weekly learning of a simple rhyme ☐

Talk

daily spoken language activities, including repeating and innovating on sentences daily ☐

targeting of selected vocabulary (changed weekly) ☐

daily targeting of PREPARE expressive language ☐

daily activities to compensate for language delay ☐

daily talk during child-initiated activities ☐

Music

regular opportunities to develop steady beat and rhythm ☐

daily opportunities to sing (and learn) songs, action songs and rhymes ☐

frequent opportunities to move rhythmically (e.g. marching, skipping, dancing) ☐

Storytime

'five a day' reading of story books ☐

frequent story-telling sessions ☐

frequent opportunities for children to join in with/recite familiar stories ☐

regular opportunities for children to make up stories ☐

Print

frequent attention to environmental print ☐

environmental print in all role-play areas ☐

gradual linking of alphabet knowledge to phonics ☐

frequent demonstration of different types of reading, in appropriate contexts ☐

encouragement of emergent reading and writing ☐

Phonics

daily rhyme, rhythm and song (link to music) ☐

daily oral activities to learn phonemes and use them to segment and blend ☐

later, daily phonic activities, using magnetic letters, etc., and eventually linking to letter formation ☐

later, integration of phonic knowledge into shared writing ☐

Writing

frequent large-scale practice of letter formation ☐

later, linking letter formation to phonics ☐

constant attention to pencil grip and handedness ☐

daily shared writing ☐

Appendix 9: *FoL* audit sheet for practitioners working with 5–6 year olds

Listening

daily activities to develop discrimination, attention span, auditory memory

   (overlap with music, storytime, phonics) ☐

weekly learning of a simple rhyme ☐

Talk

daily spoken language activities, including repeating and innovating on sentences

   (e.g. circle time, storytime) ☐

daily targeting of selected vocabulary ☐

daily targeting of PREPARE expressive language ☐

daily activities to compensate for language delay ☐

Music

daily opportunities to sing (and learn) songs, action songs and rhymes ☐

frequent opportunities to move rhythmically (e.g. marching, skipping, dancing) ☐

Storytime

'five a day' reading of story books ☐

frequent story-telling sessions, with emphasis on children's retelling of stories ☐

regular opportunities for children to make up stories orally ☐

Print

frequent attention to environmental print ☐

environmental print in all role-play areas ☐

linking of alphabet knowledge to phonics ☐

demonstration of different types of reading ☐

later (when phonics well established) sight word activities ☐

encouragement of emergent reading and writing ☐

Phonics

daily rhyme, rhythm and song (link to music) ☐

daily structured phonic activities, gradually linking to letter formation ☐

occasional reading, when children are ready, of phonically regular material ☐

integration of phonic knowledge into shared writing ☐

Writing

frequent practice of letter formation, moving from gross to fine motor control ☐

attention to pencil grip and handedness ☐

daily shared writing ☐

later, practice of writing on small whiteboards, linked to phonics and, eventually, sight words ☐

Appendix 10: Phonics revisited

As we hope is clear from *Tuning into Sound* and *Switching on the Searchlights*, we are thoroughly in favour of the teaching of phonics 'first and fast' (see also the note at the foot of page 72), as long as the teaching is also fun and developmentally appropriate. The developmental stages listed on page 78 were described to us by Professor Margaret Snowling, the UK's foremost expert on dyslexia, and do not vary over time. Children with no awareness of rhyme and alliteration are unlikely to benefit from systematic structured phonics teaching.

In the Appendix to the *Rose Report* (2006), there is a very helpful diagram by Dr Morag Stuart, showing the interrelationship between rapid 'word recognition' (by which she means the ability to rapidly synthesize an unfamiliar word from its phonetic elements: /b/ /a/ /sh/ → 'bash') and language comprehension (implicit in the level of children's command of spoken language). If children have good phonics skills and good spoken language they will, almost inevitably, be good readers.

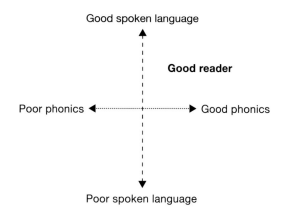

However, those children with good command of spoken language but poor phonics skills will probably fall into the trap of guessing unknown words. This is not a great handicap in the early stages of reading, as a bright child can usually make pretty effective guesses, but as time goes on and the level of vocabulary becomes more difficult, guessing doesn't work. Unfortunately, the child who has learned to guess usually finds it very difficult to slow down his or her brain sufficiently to acquire the skills of decoding.

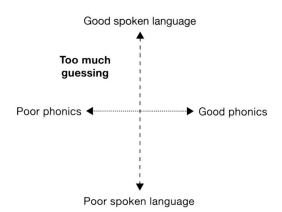

Children whose ability to discriminate phonemes is impaired for physiological reasons find it difficult to learn phonics, and – if their spoken language is good – often become inveterate guessers. These children are now said to be suffering from dyslexia. But, if phonics is not taught first and fast, children with no physiological difficulties may also learn to guess, and may be unwilling to slow down their brains at a later date to learn to decode – we could call this 'acquired dyslexia'. It is likely that, in the recent past, when phonics was taught sketchily or inappropriately (or not taught at all), many children – especially boys – suffered from acquired dyslexia. It's therefore essential that, to avoid the artificial creation of reading problems, we ensure that children are taught phonics, and taught it well, before being asked to 'orchestrate the searchlights' for reading and writing.

On the other hand, if a child has poor spoken language but good phonic knowledge, he or she will be able to decode but without comprehension. As it's impossible truly to 'read' a text without understanding its meaning, this child will struggle in literacy lessons and will usually lose interest in the activity. This used to happen regularly in the 1960s and 70s when phonics was taught thoroughly, and the children concerned were said to be 'barking at print'.

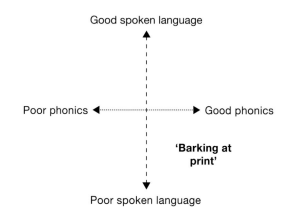

Indeed, it was because so many children from less advantaged homes were found to be 'barking at print' that confidence in phonics as a teaching method waned, and phonics was thrown out of favour in the late 70s and 1980s. There is a strong possibility that, unless we concentrate on the development of speaking and listening skills as well as phonics, these children will again fail to make adequate progress in reading.

In Scotland, where several local authorities have been teaching systematic synthetic phonics for several years, many 11 year olds from disadvantaged homes do not progress beyond a 9-year-old reading level, even on a phonic test – i.e. they are not independent readers. (Interestingly, children who started school early and were thus subjected to phonics teaching from the age of 4 often do not even attain 9-year-old levels of competence by their eleventh year – as one headteacher put it 'they seem to be inevitably among the failures'.)

The most comprehensive failures, of course, are the children who have neither well-developed spoken language nor phonic skill. They need early identification and special needs input.

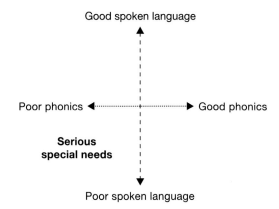

Given that practitioners are aware of the complex relationship between phonics and proficiency in spoken language (and the overarching importance of developing language competence as a whole), we believe the points listed below are essential if children are to become proficient in literacy skills.

One very important point – not clearly stated in our previous edition or in the *Rose Report* – is that you can teach **phonics for reading** without expecting children to write the letters. This releases them from the extra physical and cognitive load of wielding a pencil, and gives time to develop pencil control before revising phonic knowledge through the kinaesthetic channel at a later date.

Preparing for phonics

Children must be able to discriminate the phonemes of English in order to read.

Babies are born with the potential to speak any language, but during the first year or so their ears tune into the sounds of their mother tongue, and they become less able to discriminate other sounds. (That's why it's so difficult for Chinese people to pronounce the 'r' sound, which we take for granted – their brains have screened it out of their phonological range.)

So before children start learning to read, they need lots of exposure to spoken language, to ensure they can discriminate all the sounds – and, in terms of phonics, the first couple of years is very important. Three steps you can take to help this along are:

- Make sure parents know the huge importance of talking to their babies. There are free downloadable parents' advice sheets on www.talktoyourbaby.org, an excellent website run by the National Literacy Trust.

- Encourage parents to sing the old nursery rhymes, which emphasize specific sounds (**J**ack and **J**ill, **R**ing a **R**ing a **R**oses). The reason they've come down through the centuries is that they *work*.

- If you're in contact with local Sure Start units and day nurseries make sure they know the huge importance of talking, singing and rhyming with small children.

Phonics for reading

Children have to **decode** words when they read. A 'phonics first, fast and fun' approach prepares them to do this with relative ease.

Reading an alphabetic language like English involves two key phonic skills:

- knowing that letters (and groups of letters, such as *ch* and *igh*) represent phonemes
- segmenting words into phonemes (/k/ /a/ /t/) and blending them back into words (*cat*).

There's growing evidence that the best approach is to teach phonics **before** starting children on formal reading instruction. But that doesn't mean starting phonics earlier – it means putting off formal reading until later. There are many other important elements in an early years curriculum – including the other six strands of *FoL* – so please don't start phonics teaching until you know children are ready to benefit from it. The key messages in our *Tuning into Sound* chapter are:

- Ensure plenty of preliminary phonological and phonemic awareness activities (see pages 78–80) – these should also continue alongside phonics teaching.
- A 'phonics first, fast and fun' approach, using games and concrete materials, will then develop key phonic skills (but remember to keep it within the context of good early years practice).
- If something stops being fun, stop doing it! Find another way.
- Don't confuse children by simultaneously teaching sight words or other reading skills – get the phonics in first (see page 99).
- Read to children (you can't do enough of this) but save shared and guided reading and reading schemes until you've established the key phonic skills.
- Teach phonics in short sharp bursts (no more than a total of twenty minutes in a single day) which are fun, fast, multisensory and **cumulative**.
- Use an established scheme or put your own together, using appropriate NLS games from *Progression in Phonics* or *Playing with Sounds* – but be sure to cover the phonemes systematically, with plenty of repetition.
- Do use your professional judgement about what is appropriate for particular children – if a child is not developmentally ready to learn from an activity, it will do more harm than good.

Time spent laying the phonic foundations for reading pays off. Good phonic skills make reading 'easy', so children are more likely to succeed and make rapid progress. Explain this to parents if they start hankering for reading books – *Flying Start with Literacy* by Ros Bayley and Lynn Broadbent should be helpful here. We think Year 1 is quite early enough to start shared, guided and independent reading.

Phonics for writing

Children need to **encode** words when they write. As English spelling is so complex, phonics for writing takes a long time to teach.

Writing involves a much wider range of skills, concepts and cognition than reading (including hand-eye co-ordination and fine motor control, which are very demanding for young children, especially boys). Pre-writing skills can be developed alongside 'phonics for reading'.

When children are ready for writing (research suggests 6 is the best age), it's an ideal opportunity to revisit phonics – this time from the point of view of encoding. The original NLS framework for Years 1 and 2 make a lot of sense for teaching phonics for writing. The following are the main points to remember:

- When teaching 'phonics for reading', don't expect children to write letters. Instead, prepare for handwriting with something like *Write Dance* (Lucky Duck Publishing), separate from phonic activities.
- In Reception, demonstrate how phonics helps you transcribe words during Shared Writing, but save guided and independent writing until Year 1 when children are physically mature enough to do it comfortably.

- In Reception, children's developing grasp of phonics should show through in emergent writing (during role play, in the writing corner, etc.) – praise them for this, but don't wait for it to happen before teaching phonics. At this stage, phonics is for reading.
- In Year 1, revise phonics through the teaching of handwriting and start teaching phonics for spelling, possibly using a scheme like *Penpals* (Cambridge University Press).

Phonic problems

Children who have problems with phonics can often be helped through early identification and phonological training.

Research suggests most reading difficulties are caused by faulty phonological processing, due to neurological problems (often genetic) or inadequate language exposure in very early childhood. The *Learning to listen* and *Music, movement and memory* strands of *FoL* are therefore very important for phonics.

Schools need to spot problems and provide appropriate help *before* children fail at reading and fall behind. This is another good reason for putting off formal reading instruction until children are in Year 1. Ways of putting this research into practice are in their infancy, but key points seem to be:

- When you start phonics in Reception, watch for children who don't catch on as fast as the rest of the class, especially in 'segmenting and blending'.
- These children need screening for specific phonological problems. They are likely to benefit from intensive, individual help
  - to identify the phonemes they cannot discriminate
  - to train them to hear these sounds and link them to letters.

Dr Peter Hatcher's *Reading Intervention* programme, which is being trialled in Cumbria, may offer a way ahead.

Sue Palmer, Summer 2007

Practice Guidance for the Early Years Foundation Stage and *FoL*

In the EYFS goals for 30–50 months are shown here by dashes and early learning goals are shown by bullet points. The guidance has been colour coded to the *FoL* rainbow.

Personal, social and emotional development

Dispositions and attitudes

- seek and delight in new experiences
- have a positive approach to activities and events
- show confidence in linking up with others for support and guidance
- show increasing independence in selecting and carrying out activities
- display high levels of involvement in activities
- persist for extended periods of time at an activity of their choosing
- continue to be interested, excited and motivated to learn
- be confident to try new activities, initiate ideas and speak in a familiar group
- maintain attention, concentrate, and sit quietly when appropriate

Self-confidence and self-esteem

- show increasing confidence in new situations
- talk freely about their home and community
- take pleasure in gaining more complex skills
- have a sense of personal identity
- express needs and feelings in appropriate ways
- have an awareness and pride in self as having own identity and abilities
- respond to significant experiences, showing a range of feelings when appropriate
- have a developing awareness of their own needs, views and feelings, and be sensitive to the needs, views and feelings of others
- have a developing respect for their own cultures and beliefs and those of other people

Making relationships

- feel safe and secure, and show a sense of trust
- form friendships with other children
- demonstrate flexibility and adapt their behaviour to different events, social situations and changes in routine
- value and contribute to own well-being and self-control
- form good relationships with adults and peers
- work as part of a group or class, taking turns and sharing fairly, understanding that there needs to be agreed values and codes of behaviour for groups of people, including adults and children, to work together harmoniously

Behaviour and self-control

- begin to accept the needs of others, with support
- show care and concern for others, for living things and the environment
- show confidence and the ability to stand up for own rights
- have an awareness of the boundaries set, and of behavioural expectations in the setting

● understand what is right, what is wrong and why

● consider the consequences of their words and actions for themselves and others

Self-care

- show willingness to tackle problems and enjoy self-chosen challenges
- demonstrate a sense of pride in own achievement
- take initiatives and manage developmentally appropriate tasks
- operate independently within the environment and show confidence in linking up with others for support and guidance
- appreciate the need for hygiene

● dress independently and manage their own personal hygiene

● select and use activities and resources independently

Sense of community

- make connections between different parts of their life experience
- have an awareness of, and an interest in, cultural and religious differences
- have a positive self-image, and show that they are comfortable with themselves
- enjoy joining in with family customs and routines

● understand that people have different needs, views, cultures and beliefs, that need to be treated with respect

● understand that they can expect others to treat their needs, views, cultures and beliefs with respect

Communication, language and literacy

Language for communication

- use simple statements and questions often linked to gestures
- use intonation, rhythm and phrasing to make their meaning clear to others
- join in with repeated refrains and anticipate key events and phrases in rhymes and stories
- listen to stories with increasing attention and recall
- describe main story settings, events and principal characters
- listen to others in one-to-one or small groups when conversation interests them
- respond to simple instructions
- question why things happen and give explanations
- use vocabulary focused on objects and people that are of particular importance to them

- begin to experiment with language describing possession
- build up vocabulary that reflects the breadth of their experiences
- begin to use more complex sentences
- use a widening range of words to express or elaborate on ideas
- have confidence to speak to others about their own wants and interests
- use talk to gain attention and sometimes use action rather than talk to demonstrate or explain to others
- initiate conversation, attend to and take account of what others say
- extend vocabulary, especially by grouping and naming
- use vocabulary and forms of speech that are increasingly influenced by their experience of books
- link statements and stick to a main theme or intention
- consistently develop a simple story, explanation or line of questioning
- use language for an increasing range of purposes
- use simple grammatical structures

● interact with others, negotiating plans and activities and taking turns in conversation
● enjoy listening to and using spoken and written language, and readily turn to it in their play and learning
● sustain attentive listening, responding to what they have heard with relevant comments, questions or actions
● listen with enjoyment, and respond to stories, songs and other music, rhymes and poems and make up their own stories, songs, rhymes and poems
● extend their vocabulary, exploring the meanings and sounds of new words
● speak clearly and audibly with confidence and control and show awareness of the listener

Language for thinking

- talk activities through, reflecting on and modifying what they are doing
- use talk to give new meanings to objects and actions, treating them as symbols for other things
- use talk to connect ideas, explain what is happening and anticipate what might happen next
- use talk, actions and objects to recall and relive past experiences
- begin to use talk instead of action to rehearse, reorder and reflect on past experience, linking significant events from own experience and from stories, paying attention to how events lead into one another
- begin to make patterns in their experience through linking cause and effect, sequencing, ordering and grouping
- begin to use talk to pretend imaginary situations

● use language to imagine and recreate roles and experiences
● use talk to organize, sequence and clarify thinking, ideas, feelings and events

Linking sounds and letters

- – enjoy rhyming and rhythmic activities
- – show awareness of rhyme and alliteration
- – recognize rhythm in spoken words
- – continue a rhyming string
- – hear and say the initial sound in words and know which letters represent some of the sounds
- ● hear and say sounds in words in the order in which they occur
- ● link sounds to letters, naming and sounding the letters of the alphabet
- ● use their phonic knowledge to write simple regular words and make phonetically plausible attempts at more complex words

Reading

- – listen to and join in with stories and poems, one-to-one and also in small groups
- – begin to be aware of the way stories are structured
- – suggest how the story might end
- – show interest in illustrations and print in books and print in the environment
- – handle books carefully
- – know information can be relayed in the form of print
- – hold books the correct way up and turn pages
- – understand the concept of a word
- – enjoy an increasing range of books
- – know that information can be retrieved from books and computers
- ● explore and experiment with sounds, words and texts
- ● retell narratives in the correct sequence, drawing on language patterns of stories
- ● read a range of familiar and common words and simple sentences independently
- ● know that print carries meaning and, in English, is read from left to right and top to bottom
- ● show an understanding of the elements of stories, such as main character, sequence of events and openings, and how information can be found in non-fiction texts to answer questions about where, who, why and how

Writing

- – sometimes give meaning to marks as they draw and paint
- – ascribe meanings to marks that they see in different places
- – begin to break the flow of speech into words
- – use writing as a means of recording and communicating
- ● use their phonic knowledge to write simple regular words and make phonetically plausible attempts at more complex words
- ● attempt writing for different purposes, using features of different forms such as lists, stories and instructions

- write their own names and other things such as labels and captions, and begin to form simple sentences, sometimes using punctuation

Handwriting

- – use one-handed tools and equipment
- – draw lines and circles using gross motor movements
- – manipulate objects with increasing control
- – begin to use anticlockwise movement and retrace vertical lines
- – begin to form recognizable letters

- use a pencil and hold it effectively to form recognizable letters, most of which are correctly formed

Problem solving, reasoning and numeracy

Numbers as labels and for counting

- – use some number names and number language spontaneously
- – show curiosity about numbers by offering comments or asking questions
- – use some number names accurately in play
- – sometimes match number and quantity correctly
- – recognize groups with one, two or three objects
- – recognize some numerals of personal significance
- – count up to three or four objects by saying one number name for each item
- – count up to six objects from a larger group
- – count actions or objects that cannot be moved
- – begin to count beyond 10
- – begin to represent numbers using fingers, marks on paper or pictures
- – select the correct numeral to represent 1 to 5, then 1 to 9 objects
- – recognize numerals 1 to 5
- – count an irregular arrangement of up to ten objects
- – estimate how many objects they can see and check by counting them
- – count aloud in ones, twos, fives or tens
- – know that numbers identify how many objects are in a set
- – use ordinal numbers in different contexts
- – match then compare the number of objects in two sets

- say and use number names in order in familiar contexts
- count reliably up to ten everyday objects
- recognize numerals 1 to 9
- use developing mathematical ideas and methods to solve practical problems

Calculating

- begin to make comparisons between quantities
- know that a group of things changes in quantity when something is added or taken away
- match then compare the number of objects in two sets
- compare two groups of objects, saying when they have the same number
- show an interest in number problems
- separate a group of three or four objects in different ways, beginning to recognize that the total is still the same
- find the total number of items in two groups by counting all of them
- use own methods to work through a problem
- say the number that is one more than a given number
- select two groups of objects to make a given total of objects
- count repeated groups of the same size
- share objects into equal groups and count how many in each group
- ● in practical activities and discussion, begin to use the vocabulary involved in adding and subtracting
- ● use language such as 'more' or 'less' to compare two numbers
- ● find one more or one less than a number from one to ten
- ● begin to relate addition to combining two groups of objects and subtraction to 'taking away'

Shape, space and measures

- notice simple shapes and patterns in pictures
- begin to categorize objects according to properties such as shape or size
- begin to understand variations in size
- show an interest in shape and space by playing with shapes or making arrangements with objects
- show awareness of similarities in shapes in the environment
- observe and use potential language
- are beginning to understand 'bigger than' and 'enough'
- show interest in shape by sustained construction activity or by talking about shapes or arrangements
- use shapes appropriately for tasks
- begin to talk about the shapes of everyday objects
- show curiosity about and observation of shapes by talking about how they are the same or different
- match some shapes by recognizing similarities and orientation
- begin to use mathematical names for 'solid' 3D shapes and 'flat' 2D shapes, and mathematical terms to describe shapes
- select a particular named shape
- show awareness of symmetry

- find items from positional or directional clues
- order two or three items by length or height
- order two items by weight or capacity
- match sets of objects to numerals that represent the number of objects
- sort familiar objects to identify their similarities and differences, making choices and justifying decisions
- describe solutions to practical problems, drawing on experience, talking about own ideas, methods and choices
- use familiar objects and common shapes to create and recreate patterns and build models
- use everyday language related to time; order and sequence familiar events, and measure short periods of time with a non-standard unit, for example, with a sand timer
- count how many objects share a particular property, presenting results using pictures, drawings or numerals

● use language such as 'greater', 'smaller', 'heavier' or 'lighter' to compare quantities

● talk about, recognize and recreate simple patterns

● use language such as 'circle' or 'bigger' to describe the shape and size of solids and flat shapes

● use everyday words to describe position

● use developing mathematical ideas and methods to solve practical problems

Knowledge and understanding of the world

Exploration and investigation

- show curiosity and interest in the features of objects and living things
- describe and talk about what they see
- show curiosity about why things happen and how things work
- show understanding of cause/effect relations
- notice and comment on patterns
- show an awareness of change
- explain own knowledge and understanding, and ask appropriate questions of others

● investigate objects and materials by using all of their senses as appropriate

● find out about, and identify, some features of living things, objects and events they observe

● look closely at similarities, differences, patterns and change

● ask questions about why things happen and how things work

Designing and making

- investigate various construction materials
- realize tools can be used for a purpose
- join construction pieces together to build and balance
- begin to try out a range of tools and techniques safely
- construct with a purpose in mind, using a variety of resources

- use simple tools and techniques competently and appropriately
- build and construct with a wide range of objects, selecting appropriate resources and adapting their work where necessary
- select the tools and techniques they need to shape, assemble and join materials they are using

ICT

- know how to operate simple equipment
- complete a simple program on a computer
- use ICT to perform simple functions, such as selecting a channel on the TV remote control
- use a mouse and keyboard to interact with age-appropriate computer software
- find out about and identify the uses of everyday technology and use information and communication technology and programmable toys to support their learning

Time

- remember and talk about significant events in their own experience
- show interest in the lives of people familiar to them
- talk about past and future events
- develop an understanding of growth, decay and changes over time
- begin to differentiate between past and present
- use time-related words in conversation
- understand about the seasons of the year and their regularity
- make short-term future plans
- find out about past and present events in their own lives, and in those of their families and other people they know

Place

- show an interest in the world in which they live
- comment and ask questions about where they live and the natural world
- notice differences between features of the local environment
- observe, find out about and identify features in the place they live and the natural world
- find out about their environment, and talk about those features they like and dislike

Communities

- express feelings about a significant personal event
- describe significant events for family or friends
- enjoy imaginative and role play with peers
- show interest in different occupations and ways of life
- gain an awareness of the cultures and beliefs of others
- feel a sense of belonging to own community and place
- begin to know about their own cultures and beliefs and those of other people

Physical development
Movement and space

- move freely with pleasure and confidence in a range of ways, such as slithering, shuffling, rolling, crawling, walking, running, jumping, skipping, sliding and hopping
- use movement to express feelings
- negotiate space successfully when playing racing and chasing games with other children, adjusting speed or changing direction to avoid obstacles
- sit up, stand up and balance on various parts of the body
- demonstrate the control necessary to hold a shape or fixed position
- operate equipment by means of pushing and pulling movements
- mount stairs, steps or climbing equipment using alternate feet
- negotiate an appropriate pathway when walking, running or using a wheelchair or other mobility aids, both indoors and outdoors
- judge body space in relation to spaces available when fitting into confined spaces or negotiating openings and boundaries
- show respect for other children's personal space when playing among them
- persevere in repeating some actions or attempts when developing a new skill
- collaborate in devising and sharing tasks, including those which involve accepting rules
- go backwards and sideways as well as forwards
- experiment with different ways of moving
- initiate new combinations of movement and gesture in order to express and respond to feelings, ideas and experiences
- jump off an object and land appropriately
- show understanding of the need for safety when tackling new challenges
- avoid dangerous places and equipment
- construct with large materials such as cartons, fabric and planks
- ● move with confidence, imagination and in safety
- ● move with control and co-ordination
- ● travel around, under, over and through balancing and climbing equipment
- ● show awareness of space, of themselves and of others

Health and bodily awareness

- show awareness of own needs with regard to eating, sleeping and hygiene
- often need adult support to meet those needs
- show awareness of a range of healthy practices with regard to eating, sleeping and hygiene
- observe the effects of activity on their bodies
- show some understanding that good practices with regard to exercise, eating, sleeping and hygiene can contribute to good health
- ● recognize the importance of keeping healthy, and those things that contribute to this
- ● recognize the changes that happen to their bodies when they are active

Using equipment and materials

- engage in activities requiring hand-eye co-ordination
- use one-handed tools and equipment
- show increasing control over clothing and fastenings
- show increasing control in using equipment for climbing, scrambling, sliding and swinging
- demonstrate increasing skill and control in the use of mark-making implements, blocks, construction sets and small-world activities
- understand that equipment and tools have to be used safely
- explore malleable materials by patting, stroking, poking, squeezing, pinching and twisting them
- use increasing control over an object, such as a ball, by touching, pushing, patting, throwing, catching or kicking it
- manipulate materials to achieve a planned effect
- use simple tools to effect changes to the materials
- show understanding of how to transport and store equipment safely
- practise some appropriate safety measures without direct supervision
- use a range of small and large equipment
- handle tools, objects, construction and malleable materials safely and with increasing control

Creative development

Being creative – responding to experiences, expressing and communicating ideas

- use language and other forms of communication to share the things they create, or to indicate personal satisfaction or frustration
- explore and experience using a range of senses and movement
- capture experiences and responses with music, dance, paint and other materials or words
- develop preferences for forms of expression
- talk about personal intentions, describing what they were trying to do
- respond to comments and questions, entering into dialogue about their creations
- make comparisons and create new connections
- respond in a variety of ways to what they see, hear, smell, touch and feel
- express and communicate their ideas, thoughts and feelings by using a widening range of materials, suitable tools, imaginative and role play, movement, designing and making, and a variety of song and musical instruments

Exploring media and materials

- begin to be interested in and describe the texture of things
- explore colour and begin to differentiate between colours
- differentiate marks and movement on paper
- use their bodies to explore texture and space

- – understand that they can use lines to enclose a space, and then begin to use these shapes to represent objects
- – create 3D structures
- – begin to construct, stacking blocks vertically and horizontally, making enclosures and creating spaces
- – explore what happens when they mix colours
- – choose particular colours to use for a purpose
- – understand that different media can be combined to create new effects
- – experiment to create different textures
- – create constructions, collages, painting and drawings
- – use ideas involving fitting, overlapping, in, out, enclosure, grids and sun-like shapes
- – work creatively on a large or small scale
- – explore colour, texture, shape, form and space in two or three dimensions

Creating music and dance

- – enjoy joining in with dancing and ring games
- – sing a few familiar songs
- – sing to themselves and make up a simple song
- – tap out simple repeated rhythms and make some up
- – export and learn how sounds can be changed
- – imitate and create movement in response to music
- – begin to build a repertoire of songs and dances
- – explore the different sounds of instruments
- – begin to move rhythmically
- ● recognize and explore how sounds can be changed, sing simple songs from memory, recognize repeated sounds and sound patterns and match movements to music

Developing imagination and imaginative play

- – notice what adults do, imitating what is observed and then doing it spontaneously when the adult is not there
- – use available resources to create props to support role play
- – develop a repertoire of actions by putting a sequence of movements together
- – engage in imaginative play and role play based on their own first-hand experiences
- – introduce a storyline or narrative into their play
- – play alongside other children who are engaged in the same theme
- – play cooperatively as part of a group to act out a narrative
- ● use their imagination in art and design, music, dance, imaginative and role play, and stories

Further reading

Babytalk, Sally Ward, New Century (2000)

Basic Timing and Child Development, Kristyn Kuhlman and Lawrence J. Schweinhart, High/Scope Educational Research Foundation, Ypsilanti, Michigan, USA

Curriculum Guidance for the Foundation Stage, DfES (2002)

Developing Early Writing, DfES (2002)

Educating Young Children, Mary Hohmann and David P. Weikart, High/Scope Educational Research Foundation, Ypsilanti, Michigan, USA (2002)

Effective Provision of Pre-school Education (EPPE) part of *Researching Effective Pedagogy in the Early Years*, Iram Siraj-Blatchford and Kathy Sylva (www.DfES.gov.uk/research)

Exploring Writing and Play in the Early Years, Nigel Hall and Anne Robinson, David Fulton (2003)

Learning in the Early Years, ed. Jeni Riley, Paul Chapman Publications (2003)

Learning Language and Loving It, Elaine Weitzman, The Hanen Centre, Toronto, Canada (1992)

Literacy: What Works? Sue Palmer and Pie Corbett, Nelson Thornes (2003)

Music and the Mind, Anthony Storr, Harper Collins (1997)

Playing with Sounds, DfES (2004)

Progression in Phonics, DfES (2000)

Researching Effective Pedagogy in the Early Years, Iram Siraj-Blatchford and Kathy Sylva (DfES Research Report 356 (2002)

Supporting Language and Literacy Development in the Early Years, Marian Whitehead, Open University Press (1999)

Supporting Musical Development in the Early Years, Linda Pond and Chris Harrison, Open University Press (2002)

The Boy Who Would Be a Helicopter and other books, Vivian Gussin Paley, Harvard University Press

The Cradle of Thought, Peter Hobson, Macmillan (2002)

The Education of Six-Year-Old Children in England, Denmark and Finland, Ofsted (2003)

The Power of Fantasy in Early Learning, Jenny Tyrrell, Routledge Falmer (2001)

The Scientist in the Crib: What Early Learning Tells us About the Mind, Alison Gopnik, Andrew N Meltzoff, Patricia K Kuhl, Harper Collins (1999)

Too Much Too Soon, video giving overview of European early years practice, Clare and David Mills (1998). Available from Clare@millsproductions.demon.co.uk

Toxic Childhood: How the Modern World is Damaging our Children and What We Can do About It, Sue Palmer, Orion (2006)

Recommended resources

The resources recommended below have been used successfully in schools trialling *Foundations of Literacy* or are recommended by practitioners.

Chapter 1: Learning to listen

Circle Time for the Very Young and other circle time resources, Lucky Duck Publishing (tel: 0117 973 2881 website: www.luckyduck.co.uk)

Foundations of Literacy teaching packs by Sue Palmer and Pie Corbett, based on Cbeebies *Razzledazzle* programmes and *Listen and Play* radio series, BBC School Shop (tel: 0870 830 8000 website: bbcschoolshop.com)

Helping Young Children to Listen and *Helping Young Children to Concentrate,* Ros Bayley and Lynn Broadbent, Lawrence Educational Publications (tel: 01922 643833 website: www.educationalpublications.com)

Language through Listening, Judith Carey and *Visual Cue Cards* – 12 page pack, Black Sheep Press (tel: 01535 631356 website: www.blacksheep-epress.com)

Makaton symbols and signs (website: www.makaton.org)

Maths Call – Year R/Year 1, Developing Children's Listening Skills in the Daily Maths Lesson, HarperCollins (tel: 0870 787 1610 website: www.collinseducation.com)

Picture Communication System pictures and symbols, Mayer-Johnson, Inc. (P.O. Box 1579, Solana Beach, CA 92075–7579 USA tel: 800–588–4548 or 858–550–0084; fax: 858–550–0449 website: www.mayer-johnson.com)

The Little Book of Listening, Clare Beswick, Featherstone Education (tel: 01858 881212 website: www.featherstone.uk.com)

There are many games on the market (using ready-made taped sounds) such as: *Picture Sound Lotto* for age 4–8 (LDA tel: 01223 357788 website: www.ldalearning.com), *Soundtracks* for age 3–6 (Living and Learning tel: 01223 864886 website: www.livingandlearning.com)

For parents: *Talk to your Baby,* National Literacy Trust (tel: 020 7828 2435 website: www.literacytrust.org.uk)

Chapter 2: Time to talk

A Corner to Learn, Neil Griffiths, Nelson Thornes (tel: 01242 267280 website: www.nelsonthornes.co.uk)

Circle Time for the Very Young and other circle time resources, Lucky Duck Publishing (tel: 0117 973 2881 website: www.luckyduck.co.uk)

Feeling spinners/circle time sentence starts / barrier game materials / masks and puppets / feely bags, etc. TTS catalogue (tel: 0800 318686 website: www.tts-group.co.uk)

First Hand Experience: What Matters to Children – An Alphabet of Learning From the Real World, Diane Rich, Denise Casanova, Annabelle Dixon, Mary Jane Drummond, Andrea Durrant and Cathy Myer, Rich Learning Opportunities (website: www.richlearningopportunities.co.uk)

Helping Young Children to Speak with Confidence, Ros Bayley, Lynn Broadbent and Andrina Flinders; *Lines of Enquiry* and the *Dogum* thinking skills books, Ros Bayley and Lynn Broadbent, Lawrence Educational Publications (tel: 01922 643833 website: www.educationalpublications.com)

Here We Go Round and other titles – circle time games, Positive Press (tel: 01225 719204 website: www.circle-time.co.uk)

Just Imagine, Robina Beckles Willson and Lyn Gray, Belair Publications (tel: 0870 609 1237 website: www.folens.com)

Launch into Literacy with Alien and Ug, Ros Bayley and Lynn Broadbent, Philip & Tacey (tel: 01264 332171 website: www.philipandtacey.co.uk)

Little Book of Prop Boxes for Role Play and other little books, Featherstone Books (tel: 01858 881212 website: www.featherstone.uk.com)

Nursery Narrative Pack and *Reception Narrative Pack*, Judith Carey, Black Sheep Press (tel: 01535 631356 website: www.blacksheep-epress.com)

Makaton symbols and sign (website: www.makaton.org)

Puppets at Large, Linda Bentley, Positive Press (tel: 01225 719204 website: www.circle-time.co.uk)

Spirals: Language Development (for children with language delay), Marion Nash and Jackie Lowe, David Fulton Books (tel: 020 8996 3622 website: www.fultonpublishers.co.uk)

Storyboxes and *25 Exciting Things to do with a Builder's Tray*, Helen Bromley, Lawrence Educational Publications (tel: 01922 643833 website: www.educational publications.com)

Talking Cards: Talking with Twinkle, Ros Bayley and Lynn Broadbent, Lawrence Educational Publications (tel: 01922 643833 website: www.educationalpublications.com)

Talk to Me and other materials, Basic Skills Agency (tel: 020 7405 4017 website: www.basic-skills.co.uk)

Time to Talk, Alison Schroeder, LDA (tel: 01223 357788 website: www.ldalearning.com)

Chapter 3: Music, movement and memory

Carousel (CD), songs for developing language skills (CD and information on music workshops: Linda Caroe 01323 734418)

CBeebies songs and music (website: www.bbc.co.uk/cbeebies/singasong)

Helping Young Children to Learn through Movement, Celia O'Donovan, Lawrence Educational Publications (tel: 01922 643833 website: www.educationalpublications.com)

Helping Young Children with Steady Beat, Ros Bayley and Lynn Broadbent, Lawrence Educational Publications (tel: 01922 643833 website: www.educationalpublications.com)

JABADAO: Centre for the Study of Movement, Learning and Health (Branch House, 18 Armley Road, Armley, Leeds LS12 3AQ website: www.jabadao.org)

Music Express Foundation Stage (Developing Basic Music Skills); *Three Tapping Teddies*, etc. (stories with music activities); *Tom Thumb's Musical Maths* and many other titles, A & C Black (tel: 01256 302692 website: www.acblack.com)

Music in Action with Big Books, Gaunt and Dumville, Lovely Music (tel: 01937 832946 website: www.lovelymusic.co.uk)

Musical Leaps and Bounds (CD-ROM), Brilliant Computing, Granada Learning (tel: 0161 827 2927 website: www.granada-learning.com)

Sounds Like Playing, Margery Ouvry, Early Education (website: www.early-eduction.org.cuk)

The Little Book of Music, Featherstone Education (tel: 01858 881212 website: www.featherstone.uk.com)

The Music Maker's Approach, Hannah Mortimer (inclusive pre-school activities: NASEN tel: 01827 311500 website: www.nasen.org.uk)

Time to Sing (CD), Black Sheep Press (tel: 01535 631356 website: www.blacksheep-epress.com)

Chapter 4: Storytime!

Big book story maps, masks, storyboxes, timelines and other resources, TTS catalogue (tel: 0800 318686 website: www.tts-group.co.uk)

Music in Action with Big Books, Gaunt and Dumville, Lovely Music (tel: 01937 832946 website: www.lovelymusic.co.uk)

Puppet Talk, Lillian Coppock, Belair Publications (tel: 0870 609 1237 website: www.folens.com)

Simply the Best: Books for 0–7 Years, Ann Lazim and Sue Ellis, CLPE (tel: 020 7401 3382 website: www.clpe.co.uk)

Speaking and Listening through Narrative, Becky Shanks, Black Sheep Press (tel: 01535 631356 website: www.blacksheep-epress.com)

Storylines (book) and *Angel and Friends* (video) – ideas for using large puppets in story-telling activities, Ros Bayley and Lynn Broadbent, Lawrence Educational Publications (tel: 01922 643833 website: www.educationalpublications.com)

Storysacks materials, Neil Griffiths, Storysacks Ltd (tel: 0161 763 6232 website: www.storysack.com)

The Bumper Book of Story Telling into Writing at Key Stage 1, Pie Corbett, Clown Publishing

The Little Book of Story-telling, Mary Medlicott, Featherstone Education (tel: 01858 881212 website: www.featherstone.uk.com)

Chapter 5: Learning about print

A Corner to Learn, Neil Griffiths, Nelson Thornes (tel: 01242 267280 website: www.nelsonthornes.co.uk)

Early Vision videos for roleplay, Sue Marshall (tel: 01989 567353 website: www.earlyvision.co.uk)

Real Life Print Signs, and Symbols by Sue Palmer, TTS catalogue (tel: 0800 318686 website: www.tts-group.co.uk)

Role Play Print Packs, Sue Palmer – garage, vet, doctor, post office, café, airport, TTS catalogue, as above.

Writing Through Role Play, Lesley Clarke, Sound Learning (tel: 01543 467787)

Chapter 6: Tuning into sound

Bingo Lingo (songs and rhymes), Helen McGregor, A & C Black (tel: 01256 302692 website: www.acblack.com)

Kingfisher Playtime Treasury (playground rhymes and games), Pie Corbett, Kingfisher (tel: 020 7903 9999 website: www.kingfisherpub.com)

Literacy: What Works? Sue Palmer and Pie Corbett, Nelson Thornes (tel: 01242 267280 website: www.nelsonthornes.co.uk)

Letters and Sounds, DfES (tel: 0845 6022260 website: www.dfes.gov.uk)

Phonemic Awareness in Young Children (excellent games for developing phonemic awareness), Marilyn Jager Adams et al, Brookes Publishing (website: www.pbrookes.com)

Rhymes (activities around well-known rhymes), Rhona Whiteford, Belair Publications (tel: 0870 609 1237 website: www.folens.com)

Sue Palmer's Synthetic Phonix, Sue Palmer, Philip & Tacey (tel: 01264 332171 website: www.philipandtacey.co.uk)

The Phonics Handbook (known as 'Jolly Phonics'), Sue Lloyd, Jolly Learning (tel: 020 8501 0405 website: www.jollylearning.co.uk)

Chapter 7: Moving into writing

Left-handed Children video, Anything Left-handed (tel: 01905 25798 – also provide catalogue of resources for left-handers website: www.lefthand-education.co.uk)

Let's go Zudio creative activities for dance and music, including CD, A & C Black (tel: 01256 302692 website: www.acblack.com)

Penpals Foundation 1 pack – CD and teaching book, Cambridge University Press (tel: 01223 312393 website: www.uk.cambridge.org/)

Reasonably priced individual whiteboards (blank/wide-lined), TTS catalogue (tel: 0800 318686 website: www.tts-group.co.uk)

Write Dance (video, CD and teacher's book) – teaching handwriting through music and movement, Raghild Oussoren Voors, Lucky Duck Publishing (tel: 0117 973 2881 website: www.luckyduck.co.uk)